The Backside Of God

And Other Occasional Sermons

John N. Brittain

CSS Publishing Company, Inc., Lima, Ohio

THE BACKSIDE OF GOD

Copyright © 2000 by
CSS Publishing Company, Inc.
Lima, Ohio

All rights reserved. No part of this publication may be reproduced in any manner whatsoever without the prior permission of the publisher, except in the case of brief quotations embodied in critical articles and reviews. Inquiries should be addressed to: Permissions, CSS Publishing Company, Inc., P.O. Box 4503, Lima, Ohio 45802-4503.

Scripture quotations are from the *New Revised Standard Version of the Bible*, copyright 1989 by the Division of Christian Education of the National Council of the Churches of Christ in the USA. Used by permission.

Library of Congress Cataloging-in-Publication Data

Brittain, John Neal.
   The backside of God: and other occasional sermons / John N. Brittain.
     p.   cm.
   ISBN 0-7880-1558-3 (pbk. : alk. paper)
   1. Sermons, American. I. Title.
BV4253.B72   2000
252—dc21   99-052794
                                                                                                      CIP

This book is available in the following formats, listed by ISBN:
   0-7880-1558-3   Book
   0-7880-1559-1   Disk
   0-7880-1560-5   Sermon Prep

PRINTED IN U.S.A.

*To Eileen, Tim, and Genevieve,
who have enabled me to see God
from many perspectives*

Table Of Contents

Foreword	7
The Backside Of God *Exodus 33:12-23* *Matthew 22:15-22*	9
The Assumption Of Discipline *Matthew 6:1-6, 16-21*	15
The Christian Journey I: The Path *Mark 1:16-20* *Romans 7:14-23*	21
The Christian Journey II: The Mountain *Psalm 30* *Exodus 24:15-18* *Mark 9:2-9*	27
The Christian Journey III: The Desert *Exodus 17:1-7* *1 Corinthians 10:1-13* *Mark 1:1-13*	33
The Christian Journey IV: The Pool *Psalm 114* *Ezekiel 47:1-12* *Acts 1:1-9* *John 4:1-30*	39
Fools For The Sake Of Christ *1 Corinthians 4:8-13*	45

Eighteen Years Is Long Enough *Jeremiah 1:4-10* *Luke 13:10-17*	51
Meeting Jesus At The Well *John 4:5-30, 39-42*	57
Something New, Something Old *Matthew 13:31-36a, 44-58* *Isaiah 49:1-6*	63
"Ascribe To The Lord The Glory Due His Name ..." *Psalm 96:8*	69
Responsiblity And Motivation *Ruth 1:16*	75
Whose Values Are Your Values? *Mark 6:53—7:8*	81
More Than Sex *Song of Solomon 2:8-16a, 8:6-7* *1 John 3:11-23* *John 15:12-17*	87
What Kind Of Love? *1 John 4:7-10*	93

Foreword

I believe in the virtues of being disciplined by a lectionary, and I have grown in my life and ministry by following the cycles of the liturgical year. I have discovered, however, in more than two decades of campus ministry that there are sometimes other needs that demand addressing (the terrifying day after parents have left their first year student at the curb) and other holy days that must be observed (Homecoming, Parents' Weekend, even Final Exam Week). I suspect that all ministries have these needs and calendars with which to contend, and I hope that some of these thoughts may be useful there as well.

These sermons have all grown out of the academic context and were first preached in Neu Chapel at the United Methodist Church related University of Evansville. Some were clearly written for special occasions: "More Than Sex" and "What Kind of Love" are wedding sermons, although I have also used them to speak about marriage outside the context of a wedding ceremony.

Others deal with issues that have particular relevance to university-aged persons but, I believe, are not limited to that group; "Eighteen Years is Long Enough" addresses the sense of dismissal many young adults sense in the community of faith and "Fools For the Sake of Christ" seeks to speak to the angst of rejection, something most of us never outgrow. "Whose Values are Your Values" deals with the perennial issue of what and who will shape our lives.

"Meeting Jesus at the Well" was molded in a series of Bible studies on the story of the Samaritan woman. One of the students in that group is now a pastor in California. "Ascribe to the Lord the Glory Due His Name ..." grew out a series of discussions on the nature of worship with the Neu Chapel Deacons, the group of student leaders who help shape our campus worship life.

I am indebted to the generations of undergraduate students who have listened, critiqued, suggested and more often than not stayed awake. I am particularly grateful to colleagues at the chapel, the Reverend W. Robb Kell, and Doctors Douglas Reed, Johnny Poon, and William Eash, who have not been stinting with suggestions and ideas. I am thankful to my wife Eileen and children Timothy and Genevieve, without whose support ministry of any kind would have been impossible.

The Backside Of God

Exodus 33:12-23; Matthew 22:15-22

Without wanting to be either flippant or blasphemous, I don't think it out of line to say that there is something a little odd about the story where Moses gets to see the *back side* of God. This is Moses, the one who went up the mountain and brought down the tablets of the law; the one at whose uplifted rod the waters of the Red Sea parted and then came back together; Moses, the person who filled more roles than any other in the Torah — prophet, priest, military leader, spiritual guide, political genius. And all Moses gets to see is the *back side of God*? This does not bode well for those of us who pick up a stick and find that we have neither a snake nor a rod in our hand — just a stick. What will we get to see of God?

Naturally the answer lies in the fact that here, as in most of life, there is more to the story. Rather than being a story of Moses getting the short end of the stick (if I may continue with my "stick" motif), it is actually a story of God's amazing grace, freely given — one in a long series of such stories.

Remember where today's reading comes in the grand scheme of things. God had heard the cry of the people of Israel in their bondage in Egypt. And recall that it was not a cry directed to Yahweh, the God of their fathers, about whom they seem to have completely forgotten. No, it was simply a cry of desperation; but a cry which God heard and to which God graciously responded. God raised up Moses who led the people out of slavery in Egypt and eventually to the Holy Mountain of Sinai where they received a gift that would enable them to live in harmony with one another and in union with God: the law. But before Moses even made it down from the mountain something had gone wrong, and according to Aaron's lame excuse, the people had thrown their gold jewelry in a fire and out popped a golden calf.

The Lord was so disappointed, God determined to destroy Israel and begin anew, but Moses averted that destruction by pleading with God to change God's mind. Exodus 33 opens with good news and bad news. Moses is to lead Israel to the Promised Land; God will even send an angel on before them to clear the way for their advance; but God will not go with them. And why not? Because of God's wrathful nature? Not really; more because of God's grace and love. You see, after the sin of the golden calf, God had become very dangerous for Israel. They were such a stiff-necked people, the Lord pointed out, that there is a very good chance that with God along they will pull some new bone-headed maneuver that would result in their destruction. It is better for them to go on alone. I have heard stories told — although I'm sure no one in this sanctuary has ever experienced such a time — when a parent would say to a child, or one spouse to another, "Just leave me alone for now. Just leave me alone." And thus saith the Lord.

When the people heard this news they were quite distressed. The loss of God's guiding presence on the journey is the equivalent of being stuck in the middle of the desert without a map — sand as far as the eye can see with no apparent way out. So God is again petitioned by Moses, in today's lesson.

There are two parts to this prayer that are of key importance to us as Christians. These two movements display a pattern of spiritual awareness which have been shown and re-shown throughout history and, unless I miss my guess, are present in most, if not all, of us. The first part is that we must begin our relationship with God by admitting that before we ever acknowledge the importance of God in our lives, God knows us and has been gracious to us. For Moses, it is a matter of recalling how God, in God's grace, reached out to the Hebrew people when they did not know God and how God called Moses when Moses did not know God. For us as Christians it is a matter, as the Apostle Paul put it, that "while we were yet sinners, Christ died for our sins." God has acted on our behalf even before we were born, by providing the model of faithfulness and obedience that enables us to live in right relationship with God.

The second part is that once we, like Moses, have established and acknowledged our utter dependence on God and God's grace, our prayers become more and more personal and in the process of spiritual growth, we gain new insights into the meaning of God's grace and love. Look at the three-fold progression in Moses' petitions: "Show me your ways" (v. 13), "Go with us" (v. 16), and "Show me your glory, I pray" (v. 18). Moses asks, first, for a road map, some specific directions for living, then for God's divine presence with him and finally, for a spiritual experience which will give him new insight into God.

The request for a road map had already been fulfilled, of course, in the law. In the Old Testament, the law is never understood as an odious burden to be born, but as God's gracious gift that shows the people God's ways, how we may and ought to live in harmony with the God who loves us and whom we love. But the problem with the law is that like any gift it does put something of an onus on us. I am surely not the only one who has received gifts over the years that I really don't know what to do with: the unworn tie, the somewhat too-colorful shirt, the clock in the shape of a bird that stays in the attic. As Paul wrote to the Galatians, in the absence of a living relationship with God, we may not know exactly what to do with the gift of the law. Trying to rely on mere obedience to the law in order to win God's favor can become a liability rather than an asset.

It is this business of living by the letter of the law, by legalism, rather than in a living relationship with God that lies at the heart of the familiar Gospel lesson for today. The trap laid for Jesus was a simple one, designed to be a no-win situation. If Jesus said it was okay to pay taxes, he would lose face with the masses, who deeply and passionately resented the Roman presence and domination; if he said it was wrong to pay taxes, he would take the side of those revolutionary types who, for political and religious reasons, advocated rejection of Roman authority and even rebellion against the empire. But Jesus turned the tables.

There was more than one kind of coin available for use in first-century Judea. There were the standard Roman coins, minted with the likeness of the emperor. They held the inscription, "Tiberius,

Caesar, son of the divine Augustus" or "Tiberius, Caesar, the majestic son of God." Both the image, understood to be a violation of the second commandment prohibiting idols, and the language were clearly offensive to pious Jews. But there were other coins, coins depicting sheaves of wheat rather than the emperor's head, available which allowed them to avoid blasphemy and contamination.

When Jesus asked his examiners for a coin, without second thoughts they brought out a Roman coin with Caesar's head. The coin itself declared that they had given in to political compromise. So Jesus told them if they enjoyed the comforts of Rome, they should pay their dues to Rome.

After all, who establishes the boundaries to which the emperor's claims extend, the extent to which we allow the dominant culture to mold who we are as people? Who indeed if not we ourselves? If we make compromises that make life a little more comfortable, a little less problematic, that is our business, but we shouldn't then haul God in as the backer of some point for our own convenience in the compromise. That is a misuse and a misunderstanding of what the gift of the law is all about, a misdirected legalism. Gratitude is not a matter of trying to twist the law to fit our own purposes; it is a matter of being enabled to see things God's way.

When we recognize the amazing grace of God, when we appreciate the road map God provides as a way of molding our lives, not a means of manipulating God, we naturally want to know more of God, partly because we recognize how much there is that we don't know. And that brings us back to Moses' request to see God's glory and his chance to see the back side of God. In his *Life of Moses*, the early church father, Gregory of Nyssa, says that the reason Moses was permitted only to see God's back is that that is the proper view of one who follows, of a disciple. Seeing the back side of God is, thus, not only not a slight, it is a beautiful metaphor of the wonderful privilege of being able to follow our God.

Gregory's image contrasts the desires of the people in Exodus 32 to *have an experience with* God and Moses' desire in Exodus 33 *to know* God. Aaron and Company proceeded with the time-honored practice of trying to manipulate and control God, making an idol; but Moses asked God for a meeting. Some modern Christians of all stripes — liberals, conservatives, Protestants, Catholics — seem especially certain that they not only know God's will on a whole range of issues — economics, sexual ethics, and politics (all of which get intertwined) — but feel quite assured that God must validate their positions.

In a recent discussion group a student gave a 1990s kind of definition of religious dialogue: tell me what you think, so I can explain to you how wrong you are. Unfortunately, many of us seem to mistake hard language and hard-heartedness with being tough-minded and committed. The Pharisees who confronted Jesus talked tough but were really self-absorbed. Moses was totally committed to serving God and God's people, and the best he got was a glimpse of the back side of God. But that is not a bad view for all of us. It is a view that fosters humility, and that reminds us that God leads us, we do not control God.

The Assumption Of Discipline

Matthew 6:1-6, 16-21

You don't need to be told that we live in a superficial society. We (at least men) surf the channels on the television, catching a glimpse of multiple shows without really watching any one in depth. Increasing numbers of us are doing the same with the internet, confusing access to multiple sources of information for comprehension of it. We are obsessed with physical appearance, creating a massive cosmetic surgery industry while many Americans lack basic health care. It used to be a joke when Billy Crystal's Fernando character on *Saturday Night Live* would say, "It's more important to look good than it is to feel good." It ain't funny any more.

Increasingly, Americans seem to accept it as a given that public life is disconnected from personal morality, so the idea of ethical accountability for public figures or business leaders seems naive and quaint. In the justice system, the search for truth often seems to be obscured by the best game plan or the most corrupt investigators. And on and on it goes. We live in a fast paced world where we often seem to be skimming the surface of things. We assume that this is just the way things are.

The words from Matthew 6, traditionally read on Ash Wednesday to begin Lent, reveal some very different assumptions on the part of Jesus of Nazareth. He knew, of course, that life could be lived at a superficial level, concerned mostly with appearances and with what other people think of us, but he recommends something else. He recommends a *pious* life, one that not only *looks* beneath the surface but which *lives* at a deeper level. Jesus assumes that we will practice piety, and that that will include almsgiving, prayer, fasting, and prioritizing; he assumes that we will live according to some discipline, some method, that pushes us beneath the superficial.

There are those who point out — and in fact this is one reason that many Christian churches do not observe Lent, or anything like it — that the spiritual disciplines of which Jesus speaks in this passage — alms-giving, prayer, and fasting — simply reflect the Jewish religious practices of his day. They are no longer relevant for us, these Christians argue. All that is relevant for us is the spiritual change that Jesus works in my heart. In a C. S. Lewis discussion group we have seen how that great British Christian thinker approached this line of thought. "We value Shakespeare for the glory of his language and his knowledge of the human heart ..." Lewis wrote in an essay dealing with the doctrine of Christ's return to earth (*"The World's Last Night"*) "not for his belief in witches or the divine right of kings, or his failure to take a daily bath." "When we propose to ignore in a great man's teaching those doctrines which it has in common with the thought of his age," Lewis went on, "we seem to be assuming that the thought of his age was erroneous." So, with regard to today's passage, people might say that these teachings of Jesus no longer apply to us because we are not first century Palestinian Jews.

But, Lewis pointed out, if we accept the doctrine of the Incarnation, that God was fully speaking God's word through Jesus in a unique way, we need to be very cautious in suggesting that the circumstances of his life were a hampering or distorting influence. Indeed, if the word of God became incarnate in what the Apostle Paul called "the fullness of time" (Galatians 4:4), it would suggest that he believed that the timing and cultural setting were *just right* for God's will to be fully communicated. No wonder Jesus insisted, "Do not think that I have come to abolish the law or the prophets; I have come not to abolish but to fulfill" (Matthew 5:17). The law and the prophets had perfectly set the stage for Jesus' ministry. And Jesus says "whenever you give alms," "whenever you pray," "whenever you fast," not "if" or "in the event you choose to," but "whenever."

Almsgiving, charity in the modern sense of the word, is always open to abuse. It can be done in a hypocritical and self-serving manner. It can be a fertile area for graft and fraud. It was a scandal in Jesus' day as it sometimes is in ours that those charged with administering the distribution of aid to the poor (the priests and Levites in the Jerusalem Temple, for instance) often kept too much for themselves. But in spite of potential abuses, almsgiving — giving to sustain others in need — is an important part of the life of faith for at least two reasons: it reminds us that we have a responsibility to see to the welfare of others because we are all children of God; that after all there is only one class and race of people, the human race. We may create all kinds of pecking orders and hierarchies and class systems, but in God's sight we are all the same, and in the end, Jesus reminds us, it is God who is doing the important looking. Almsgiving also reminds us of our own vulnerability as persons. I grew up in Cleveland, Ohio. The home of the Cleveland Orchestra is "Severance Hall," named for the industrialist couple who were benefactors of many causes in Cleveland in the 1920s, including classical music. My mother would often comment on how, when the Great Depression struck, the Severances lost everything, including their home, and a small apartment was provided for them in the upper levels of the concert hall they had built. They ended up — at least the way Mom told the story — in worse shape than her family.

A student I am currently supervising has been researching church-related aid to the poor in Evansville and has impressively documented what I hope we all know: that the vast majority of persons in this community who are receiving aid — whether government or private — are not the stereotypical welfare cheats of political rhetoric. Most are white and either elderly, disabled, or working poor. When you meet these folks and talk with them, at a place like the inner city ministry Patchwork Central or the Evansville Rescue Mission, you realize how much we have in common. They are us and we are them. We become keenly aware that most persons who are giving aid are one short step — loss of a job, catastrophic injury or illness —away from needing it. Almsgiving, in other words, enables us to keep our perspective on the world, and to be in a right relationship with other persons.

Anybody who is serious about walking with God comes to see that prayer has to be the main business in life, because it is through prayer that we are in communication with God and become increasingly sensitive to God's will. Of course prayer can be abused: it can be a showy public display of piety or a means of self-deception as we try to convince ourselves that our selfish desires are really God's doing. But, as in the case of almsgiving, the abuses do not negate the practice. "In the morning, while it was still very dark," we read in Mark 1, "(Jesus) got up and went out to a deserted place, and there he prayed." When the apostles were tempted to invest their time and energies in other very necessary and important tasks in the exciting days of rapid expansion in the Jerusalem Christian community, they determined to give themselves continually to prayer and the ministry of the word (Acts 6:4). And Martin Luther, when asked how he managed all his affairs, declared, "I have so much business I cannot get on without spending three hours daily in prayer." John Wesley spent two hours per day. Obviously this investment in prayer is not just to praise God although it is for that; nor is it simply to ask God for mercies, while that clearly is important as well. Perhaps the most important part of prayer is to listen in God's presence, to be molded and formed by God so that we come to be more the person God intended us to be. This can bring genuine liberation and peace of mind to us. It also lays great responsibilities on us as we become more attuned to God's will for us. So if almsgiving enables us to be in a right relationship with other persons, prayer keeps us in right relationship with God.

But then what about fasting? In our culture where the landscape is dotted not with shrines of Baal nor temples of Aphrodite but by Golden Arches, fasting certainly seems out of place. Jesus says that fasting is not to be a show, and we have to remember not to confuse it with the excessive and masochistic mortification of the Middle Ages. Nor is it dieting, which has a physical motivation, nor a hunger strike which has a political or public relations focus, nor even a planned famine to raise money for the hungry, all of which are good things, but not fasting. Fasting, which is found throughout the Bible, is to abstain periodically from food in order to focus one's time, energy, and being more fully on God. But because fasting involves a sacrifice, not of time, like prayer, nor of money, like almsgiving, but of *food* it does put us more in tune with our bodies, our inspirited selves. It reminds us of what we need, as opposed to what we want, and of what is good for us rather than what tastes good.

When we look at these disciplines, which Jesus assumes believers will practice, we cannot but be struck by something. Almsgiving brings us in right relationship with other people; prayer brings us in right relationship with God; fasting brings us in right relationship with ourselves, our own bodies. Does that remind you of any Bible passage from Sunday School days? How about Mark 12:29-31: "Jesus answered, 'The first (commandment) is, "Hear, O Israel: the Lord our God, the Lord is one; you shall love the Lord your God with all your heart, and with all your soul, and with all your mind, and with all your strength." The second is this, "You shall love your neighbor as yourself." There is no other commandment greater than these.' "

The fact that virtually anyone who even toys with the idea of Christianity — and many who do not — recognize these words as the two Great Commandments but are uncomfortable with the traditional spiritual disciplines of almsgiving, prayer, and fasting shows the extent to which our Christian faith has become very superficial. We think that we can assent to the Christian ideal without living it; that we can affirm the need to be in a right relationship with God, our fellows, and ourselves and not *do* anything about it. Not so, says Jesus. "Whenever you give alms, whenever you pray, whenever you fast."

Life is a matter of priorities. We all know that. But priorities are lived, not just spoken. *Do* those things that fulfill the commandments, Jesus says. Do not store up treasures on earth, but in heaven. Set your priorities straight; *do those things* which put you in a right relationship with others, with God and with yourselves. We need them all the time, not just at Lent.

The Christian Journey I: The Path

Mark 1:16-20; Romans 7:14-23

Have you ever been lost, *really* lost? It can happen anywhere: in a dark forest where you've lost the trail or in a crowded shopping mall where you've lost sight of Mom; on the backroads of Indiana where all you can see is corn or in the bustling canyons of New York City where the buildings block out the sun. You can be lost in a foreign country where no one speaks your language and you don't speak theirs. And you can be just as lost with a group of people who just don't understand what you are trying to say. And, of course, we can be lost within ourselves. It is this sense of lostness that the Apostle Paul recorded so eloquently in the letter to the Romans:

> *I do not understand my own actions. For I do not do what I want, but I do the very thing I hate ... For I do not do the good I want, but the evil I do not want is what I do. Now if I do what I do not want, it is no longer I that do it, but sin that dwells within me. So I find it to be a law that when I want to do what is good, evil lies close at hand. For I delight in the law of God in my inmost self... wretched man that I am! Who will rescue me from this body of death?*
> — Romans 7:15, 19-22, 24

Feeling lost, not knowing where to turn, is one of the most hopeless feelings any of us can experience.

The Good News of the gospel is that there is resolution to this universal human experience of lostness, and it is found in Jesus Christ. Paul's often quoted words about lostness are not the last words, thankfully; there is another sentence in the paragraph: "Thanks be to God through Jesus Christ our Lord!" (Romans 7:25).

It is no wonder that one of the earliest — perhaps *the* earliest — designation used to describe those who were devoted to Jesus was "followers of *the way*," in Greek *hodos*, a path, a road, a highway, but a term that soon enough came to mean a way of life. Commitment to Jesus Christ, Christian discipleship presupposes, then, that we live in a world where it is not only possible to get lost in a variety of ways, but that it is likely. And it presupposes that in Jesus we find a way of life that will enable us to make our way through this world.

Christian discipleship is not an abstract philosophy or a code of beliefs: to be a Christian is to live in a certain way, to follow a certain path. How we find this path and how we stay on it — the Christian journey — is one of the fundamental motifs of discipleship. Today and for the next few weeks, I want to share some biblical images of the Christian journey — how we make our way through this world of lostness; but more than just making our way, how we mature and grow in our commitment to Jesus Christ.

There are three images of people on the way that each speak of how we follow Christ at different times in our lives. Perhaps the most familiar is the one from the Gospel lesson: "And Jesus said to them, 'Follow me and I will make you fish for people.' And immediately they left their nets and followed him" (Mark 1:18). There are times in our lives when Jesus dramatically beckons us to stop what we are doing for the moment and to make a real commitment to follow him by redirecting our lives toward him and others — fishing for people — taking our own place on the path of discipleship and helping others find theirs.

The drama of this familiar story *does not* mean, as is sometimes implied, that the call came out of nowhere and that these fishermen were gullible Gusses who would just as well have followed some lunatic looking for a spaceship behind a comet. The yearning was no less than that felt by people today who are searching anywhere for meaning in life, calling psychic hotlines and falling for every new television guru. But within Judaism at that time and place there was a high level of expectation that God would work in some new way to show God's love and compassion as

God had in the days of the patriarchs and prophets. John the Baptist in particular had prepared the way for Jesus, announcing that God was working in a particular way to reach out to humankind one more time. Furthermore, we know from John's Gospel that there had been talk among John's disciples and others about Jesus. So while the call from Jesus was dramatic, as was the response from the disciples, it was not without preparation.

But the drama of this familiar story *does mean* that the time comes when Jesus calls, and we had better follow. There are different kinds of preparations and a variety of calls. For some, church membership or confirmation training is a time of intense preparation to follow Christ; for others it may be a church camp or retreat, a special youth rally or a revival at church. But there comes that moment when the yearning and the thinking and the listening come together and we hear Jesus saying, "Follow me and I will make you fish for people." For some of you, these factors have come together and you are on the way, and you need to stay on the way; for others, you may have heard the call but, for whatever reason, are still mending nets; for others the call will come soon, maybe this morning or in a Christian group meeting or on SEARCH Retreat, maybe sitting alone in your dorm room. This image reminds us that the journey on the way must start somewhere, and after all the preparation is said and done, the time to follow comes, and we need to get moving.

But the journey does not always begin with Jesus speaking. It may just as well begin with us. Later in Mark's Gospel, there is another interesting story that is set at the side of the path.

> *As he and his disciples and a large crowd were leaving Jericho, Bartimaeus son of Timaeus, a blind beggar, was sitting by the roadside. When he heard that it was Jesus of Nazareth, he began to shout out and say, "Jesus, Son of David, have mercy on me!" Many sternly ordered him to be quiet, but he cried out even more loudly, "Son of David, have mercy on me!" Jesus stood still and said, "Call him here." And they called the blind man, saying to him, "Take heart; get up, he is calling*

> *you." So throwing off his cloak, he sprang up and came to Jesus. Then Jesus said to him, "What do you want me to do for you?" The blind man said to him, "My teacher, let me see again." Jesus said to him, "Go; your faith has made you well." Immediately he regained his sight* and followed him on the way.
>
> — Mark 10:46-52

Once again, it is obvious that some preparation had occurred, because when Bartimaeus heard that it was Jesus passing by he knew enough to cry out for help. We have no idea if he had just heard about Jesus from the crowds, or if he had long heard stories about the wonder-working rabbi from Galilee, but he had heard about Jesus from somebody, and he cried out for healing. Once again this image of Bartimaeus crying out fits many of us at various times in our lives. There are those times when we know in our minds that there has to be relief for the pain we feel, for our blindness or deafness or inability to see a direction out of a dilemma. We may even be in a crowd of believers, like that throng exiting from Jericho with Jesus, but we feel left out; we are along the side of the road, and we want to cry out, "Jesus, Son of David, have mercy on me!"

There are two things to notice about that crowd surrounding Bartimaeus. First, the positive: he heard from the crowd that Jesus was passing by. Now, the negative: the crowd told him to shut up. "Many sternly ordered him to be quiet...." This crowd behavior actually reminds me of a lot of Christians today. The church and church folks know all about Jesus and talk about him a lot, but if someone who really needs to see Jesus begins to make noise, the church can be awfully inhospitable. Too often the blind, the addicted, the troubled, and the hurting feel alienated because they really are not welcome in the church. They have a way of shouting out and letting others know about their troubles. They make the church people uncomfortable.

You may have been in this scene one way or another. Maybe you have been hurt or in pain and shouted, "How could God have allowed this to happen to me?" or just, "God, please help me if you can!" only to be told to hush up. Or maybe you've been one of the hushers and mistaken a heart-felt plea for God's mercy for doubt or disrespect. I am sure that at least some of those who chastised Bartimaeus were trying to shield Jesus from this nuisance; but this kind of nuisance was precisely the center of Jesus' ministry. God does not need to be shielded from our pain and hurt. "Immediately he regained his sight *and followed him on the way.*"

Both of these stories, the call by the seashore and blind Bartimaeus calling out to Jesus, are stories of beginnings, and that's a good place to start. But the metaphor of journey, of path, reminds us that our relationship with Jesus Christ has not only a beginning but a middle and an end — it is meant to lead somewhere. In Matthew's Gospel Jesus says that his disciples should follow him through that narrow gate "For the gate is narrow and the road is hard that leads to life, and there are few who find it" (Matthew 7:14).

The third image of a path captures two people rather far up the road, and the journey has not become any easier. On the road to Emmaus two persons, Cleopas and no doubt his wife Mary (see John 19:25), were rightfully distraught after the dreadful end of Jesus' ministry. The forces of evil had prevailed, and Jesus lay dead in the tomb, or so it seemed. But in the midst of their pain, as they struggled to make sense out of what had happened, out of what they had felt and heard and seen, the risen Christ came to them, walked with them, and opened their eyes to the real facts.

This image teaches us about the trials of the journey. The way does not become any easier, in spite of the misimpressions we may sometimes get. Indeed, if scripture is to be believed, the way often becomes more challenging as we become stronger. Peter, who so readily left his nets that day by the lake, later publicly denied Jesus, and at the hour of our Lord's greatest need all twelve disciples faltered.

But the good news is that as we progress and are challenged, we are not left alone. We too are met along the road by the resurrected Jesus in the experience of the Holy Spirit, and Jesus promised in John 14:26, "But the Advocate, the Holy Spirit, whom the Father will send in my name, will teach you everything, and remind you of all that I have said to you." As we continue on the path, as we struggle with new situations and grapple with their meaning, as did Cleopas and his companion, Christ will come to warm our hearts and open our eyes so that we can continue to grow and to encourage others to join us on the way.

The biblical metaphor of Christian journey reminds us of three things: our life as disciples has a beginning; it has a direction and a goal; and we are not there yet. Have you begun your journey with Jesus Christ? Are you making progress toward the goal? How far have you come along the way?

The Christian Journey II: The Mountain

Psalm 30; Exodus 24:15-18; Mark 9:2-9

Virtually every religion has regarded mountains as sacred places. Mircea Eliade, the great religious scholar, called mountains an *axis mundi*, a symbolic link between heaven and earth, between the divine and the human. For those of us from the flat lands of the midwest it may not be as obvious as it should be why this is so. There is something about a mountain that lifts one's mind beyond the mundane no matter how you look at it. A mountain on the horizon cannot help but move you to think of the majesty and power of nature, if not of God. It puts things into perspective and can be a symbol of strength and reassurance. From the bottom, or part way up, mountains are a sign of challenge and call for perseverance and the best effort we can muster. And then from the top! From the mountain top you gain a vista that is incomparable!

It is no wonder that mountains play all these roles in biblical religion. One of the earliest names for God, that revealed to Abraham in Genesis 17, is *el Shaddai*, traditionally translated "God Almighty," but literally, "God, the one of the mountains." A mountain is a natural image for God's power, as well as for human stability. "By your favor, O Lord, you had established me as a strong mountain" (Psalm. 30:7). Of course a mountain can also be an obstacle (Zechariah. 4:7) but God will remove all such barriers when God's redemption is complete: "every mountain and hill shall be made low" (Isaiah 40:4).

But how does the image of the mountain fit into the idea of the Christian journey, our lifetime of following Jesus Christ as Lord and Savior? One obvious way is that it reminds us, if you'll forgive me for saying so, that life has its ups and downs. The journey of Christian discipleship, being followers of Jesus Christ, is not a walk along a level path, let alone a downhill slide. It is a journey that demands commitment and effort. There is a long tradition in Christian writing of what is referred to as "ascent" literature, sometimes using the image of scaling a mountain, often of ascending a ladder, like that in Jacob's dream. This ascent literature speaks of the ways in which disciples of Jesus Christ may advance in their spiritual walk, ever moving closer to Christ. Many persons have criticized this school of writing and this sort of imagery for putting too much emphasis on human effort and constructing an artificial plan of "first you do this and then you do that" to advance to the next higher level of spiritual growth.

I personally feel that both of these objections have some validity, particularly that of underestimating the importance of our individuality. If there is one thing that the Bible makes clear it is that God has created us as individuals with different interests, abilities, and strengths, and that God works in a variety of ways to be in relationship with different people. There is no one model of the church, no one right way to pray, and no one valid method for our varied spiritual journeys.

But the image of ascending the mountain reminds us of two very important things: first that Christian discipleship takes effort, foresight, and (as the word indicates) discipline, like that exercised by a skilled mountain climber; and second, that we should never be content to stay where we are in our relationship with God, but should constantly be striving for a higher level, what John Wesley referred to as "going on to perfection." This is the same point that the apostle Paul made by using one of his favorite metaphors, that of the athlete in training, certainly a common sight in the Greek cities in which he ministered. He spoke of the runner:

> *Not that I have already obtained this or have already reached the goal; but I press on to make it my own, because Christ Jesus has made me his own. Beloved, I do not consider that I have made it my own; but this one thing I do: forgetting what lies behind and straining forward to what lies ahead, I press on toward the goal for the prize of the heavenly call of God in Christ Jesus.* — Philippians 3:12-14

and of the boxer:

> *Athletes exercise self-control in all things; they do it to receive a perishable wreath, but we an imperishable one. So I do not run aimlessly, nor do I box as though beating the air.*   — 1 Corinthians 9:25-26

This note of training, of discipline, of striving to be stronger and better every day is at the heart of virtually all Christian theology, including the great Reformation traditions, but is a theme that is often overlooked in modern American Protestant churches which seem more intent on preaching a gospel of spiritual comfort and easy success.

But if the mountain is a sign of God's strength and our need to exercise discipline in following Jesus, it is also a sign of God's great love and mercy. It is the place where we have "mountain-top experiences," those moments of revelation when life suddenly appears clearer, when things take their place, like the panoramic view from a mountain peak. It was on a mountain that God inexplicably spoke to Moses, revealing not just God's name, but God's will for a whole people and the role this shepherd was to play in God's plan. It was on a mountain that God gave the people of Israel the great gift of the law, those ten words which would lead them in the paths of righteousness and life. It was from a mountain that Jesus spoke those words that stand in such stark contrast to the world's way of looking at things:

> *Blessed are the poor in spirit, ... those who mourn, ... the meek, ... those who hunger and thirst for righteousness, ... the merciful, ... the pure in heart, ... the peacemakers.*   — Matthew 5

And it was on a mountaintop that Peter, James, and John heard perhaps the most astonishing and most grace-filled teaching of all: "This is my Son, the Beloved; listen to him!" (Mark 9:7).

These "mountaintop" experiences in the Bible stand in stark contrast to what we often think of as "peak" experiences insofar as they combine the affective and the intellectual, the emotional and the rational. Think of two of the most familiar mountain incidents in the life of Moses. In Exodus 3 he is attracted by a bush that burns without burning up. When God speaks to him he is flabbergasted, overwhelmed by a sense of unworthiness. But by the end of the encounter on the "mountain of God" he has been taught the Divine Name, received a commission for his task with the people of Israel, and been given a sign that God would accompany him. The experience was both deeply moving and intelligible. He *knew* what he had to do. In Exodus 19 and 20 Moses was on the mountain engulfed by "smoke (that) went up like the smoke of a kiln, while the whole mountain shook violently," (Exodus 19:18) all accompanied by trumpet blasts. But when he came down, he bore laws that not only could be articulated but which could be interpreted and obeyed. In these, and many other peak emotional experiences recorded in the Bible, whether or not they actually took place on a mountain, this overwhelming sense of emotion is tied to a deep understanding of the commandments and will of God. This is why Israel always understood the law as God's greatest gift, never as a burden, because following the law frees us to become the persons that God has created us to be. It releases us from the nagging doubts about how we should behave.

There is a problem in many Protestant churches today, and it is that we too often divorce these two aspects of God's grace: the emotional release and the intellectual knowledge which our journey with Christ provides. Indeed, at times we almost pit these two against one another. Some churches stress the emotion of the mountaintop experience but do little to encourage growth in the knowledge of scripture and doctrine, let alone service to God and others; everything is on the "feeling" level and every service is a big "celebration." On the other hand, there are churches which do an excellent job of teaching scripture and doctrine but which produce believers who seem to be emotionless if not downright mean. Clearly the scriptural image of the mountaintop experience shows us that our human limitations, our inclination to categorize and compartmentalize, have gotten the best of us. God after all created both lobes of our brain, and still calls us to "love the Lord your

God with all your heart, and with all your soul, and with all your mind, and with all your strength" (Mark 12:30).

There is one more very important thing of which the image of the mountain reminds us: people do not live on mountaintops. They climb there; they are inspired there; they are instructed there; and then they go back down. And, if you will recall what Moses found when he took the tablets down the first time, you'll realize that what's waiting at the foot of the mountain isn't always so hot. Who hasn't attended a particularly meaningful worship experience and then had a fight in the car on the way home? Or been picked up at church camp or from a retreat on a particular spiritual high only to have one's parents go over the litany of undone chores at home. Many times we, like Peter on the Mount of Transfiguration, want to stay at that high: "It is good for us to be here; let us make three dwellings, one for you, one for Moses, and one for Elijah." (Mark 9:5). Let's stay a while; let's keep the party going. I have known people — and I'll bet I'm not the only one — who spend virtually all their time in church or para-church activities. They aren't all ministers either. There is always one more committee, one more special service, one more campus Christian group. They pitch their dwelling and stay on the mountaintop. The trouble is, they have no life. Relationships suffer, if they exist at all. There is no outreach, no service beyond the walls of the church or the confines of the group. In the Gospel stories of the transfiguration, Jesus doesn't even answer Peter's suggestion other than to say, "Get up," and lead the three down the mountain. Mountaintops are wonderful places, but they *are not where you live.*

Do you remember the story of Elijah the prophet? After his great success at Mount Carmel against the priests of Baal, Elijah made his way back to Horeb, the mountain of God, the same place where Moses had had his experience at the bush. Elijah was no doubt looking for some rejuvenation, perhaps an experience of renewal, a reminder of God's presence with him. But twice the Lord asks Elijah the same question, "What are you doing here, Elijah?" He'd had his mountaintop experiences and now was supposed to be serving.

So back to my beginning question, how does the image of the mountain fit into the idea of the Christian journey? It fits in by reminding us of the discipline and effort that is often needed to follow Christ. It is also a sign of God's great love and mercy, the place where God powers our emotion and our intellect in "mountain-top experiences." But it is not where we live. Indeed, if we retreat to the mountaintop too often, always looking for a spiritual high, for "religious chills and thrills," the Lord may just ask us, "What are you doing here? Why are you not following your Lord among the poor, the hopeless, and the hungry?" Because when Jesus summons us to the journey, he says, "Follow me," and then goes headlong into the world.

The Christian Journey III: The Desert

Exodus 17:1-7; 1 Corinthians 10:1-13; Mark 1:1-13

Years ago I visited a university which was really in the middle of nowhere. That is to say the university was the town — except for the grain elevator and a 25 employee factory that assembled sporting goods. I had a very cordial visit and at the end of my few days there, I was driven to the nearest airport, about three hours away. The flight was late, then quite late when a crew member came in to tell me, the sole passenger getting on the plane, that it was broken and I would have to fly out in the morning, but not to worry since the airline would put me up in the airport hotel.

Everyone was very nice when I checked in. It was now evening so I asked if there was a restaurant in the hotel. No, I was told, but there was a Taco Bell down the road a piece. How could I get there? Well, it was about ten miles, and I could call a cab from town. They charged to come out to the hotel, so it would be about twenty dollars to get there and another twenty dollars to get back. I mean no offense, but I have never yet seen a Taco Bell that was worth a forty-dollar round trip. After enjoying a dinner of dry roasted peanuts, it dawned on me that I had no clean clothes for the next morning, so I went back to the front desk and asked if there was a washing machine I could use. The clerk perked up because she had the answer: "Yeah, there's a laundromat right next to Taco Bell!" At that point, I truly felt like I was in the desert, the wilderness.

It tells us something about the setting of the Bible that there are several Hebrew words used to describe the desert: *Midbar, 'Arabah, Yeshimon, Chorbah* and *Tsiyyah* among others. They all describe unproductive, rocky wastelands rather than picturesque sand dunes; places where, by and large, you don't want to be. The desert, by its nature, is a place that throws you back on your own devices, whether it is figuring how to cope without water or determining where to hang your underwear to dry. It is an inhospitable place, but a place where we sometimes find ourselves whether we want to be there or not.

You can find yourselves in the desert in all kinds of settings, not just foreign countries or midwest airports: in new communities when you have to move; or in a new school or a new job. You can find yourself in the desert when the familiar lets you down: when those you thought were your friends suddenly turn on you; when the activities that have always been exciting and rewarding don't have that old zing; when the devotional magazine or Christian group that has been such a source of inspiration suddenly leaves you cold; when you just can't seem to pray anymore. These are all desert experiences, when we find ourselves in an inhospitable and arid place, thrown back on our own devices. And when we are honest, we know that we spend a lot of time in the desert.

Fortunately a great deal of the Bible takes place in the desert too. We know that the Egypt of the book of Exodus was a fascinating place. Under the Pharaohs it was famous for its beauty and was the seat of great culture and learning. The Israelites were making bricks for marvelous building projects that would be the envy of the world. Unfortunately they couldn't enjoy much of that order and beauty because they were slaves. The desert represented for them lack of comfort, lack of control, danger, *and freedom from slavery.*

This is one great lesson that the image of the desert has to teach us. There are times in everyone's life when the moment comes to recognize those things in the comfortable and familiar that are enslaving us, that are holding us back from progressing on to become the persons that God is calling us to be — indeed willing to lead us into becoming. These need not be "bad" things, any more than the building projects in Egypt were inherently "bad." I am not talking here about getting away from vices or habitual sins (although that is a good thing to do); I am referring to *anything* that enslaves us, that holds us back from fully turning our lives over to God. Two familiar New Testament stories underscore this point. In preparation for his public ministry, the evangelists tell us "Jesus was led up by the Spirit into the wilderness" (Matthew 4:1). No one has ever implied that Jesus had some major character defect or great sin to overcome; yet he went into the wilderness to be tempted and to prepare for his great mission.

Similarly the apostle Paul tells us in the autobiographical first chapter of Galatians, that after his dramatic experience on the road to Damascus,

> *I did not confer with any human being, nor did I go up to Jerusalem to those who were already apostles before me, but I went away at once into Arabia, and afterwards I returned to Damascus. Then after three years I did go up to Jerusalem.* — Galatians 1:16b-18a

How much of that three year period was spent in the desert of Arabia is a matter of conjecture, but Paul is making it clear that he had issues to clarify, not by talking with authority figures in the church, but by consulting with God in solitude. In Paul's case, he has just told us what his problem was: again, not what we would normally think of a vice or bad habit. He suffered from misdirected religious zeal, a desire to serve God and be faithful to God that led him to persecute the early Christians whom he was convinced were blaspheming God by claiming that Jesus was God's Son. He needed to break loose of old ways of looking at things which he now saw were enslaving him from acknowledging the way that God was working through the resurrected Lord Jesus.

In the fairly obtuse passage from 1 Corinthians 10, Paul explains his understanding of the Israelites' journey through the desert. Without dismissing the literal meaning of the story as a time of wandering in the wilderness, the apostle gives a symbolic reading so that this story makes sense both in terms of his own personal experience in Arabia and as a model for all Christians. Like them, all Christians are "under the cloud," that is, led by the Holy Spirit just as the Israelites were led by the pillar of cloud by day and fire by night, led by a presence that is taking us somewhere, even if we don't know where. We are "baptized in the cloud and in the sea," baptized, as Jesus taught, by water and the spirit. We all are nourished by the same supernatural food — they all ate manna, we all share in the Eucharist, a practice Paul addresses a few verses later. And finally, the water which flowed from the rock which Moses struck was understood as a symbol of the saving acts of Jesus Christ, the living water. By the way, this passage was the inspiration for the famous hymn text, "Rock of Ages, Cleft for Me."

Paul was neither the first nor the last to understand the desert wanderings as an essential part of the life of faith. The third century theologian Origen was struck by the opening line of Numbers 33: "These are the stages by which the Israelites went out of the land of Egypt." He assumed that a deeper meaning of this scripture was to explicate the "stages" of life for everyone who leaves the familiar but binding life of Egypt and sets out for a deeper relationship, led by God. In a famous sermon he wrote that it would be downright "wicked" to read that verse as though it only had historical significance and no spiritual meaning.

Here it seems to me both Origen and Paul were getting at the same point from different directions. The desert, that inhospitable, difficult place of temptation, was the undoing of some and the proving ground for others. Many — Paul says most — of the Israelites stumbled and fell; they worshiped idols, they complained, they indulged in immoral behavior. But some of the Old Testament prophets recall that for a few it was a time of special communion with God, of receiving and meditating on the law, of trusting God for everything — literally being fed and led along the way by the Lord. And it was in that same desert that Jesus prevailed over the Devil by living out his proclamation: "One does not live by bread alone, but by every word that comes from the mouth of God" (Matthew 4:4).

Circumstances may try us but we, by God's grace, determine our response. Those who were nourished in the wilderness had no more manna to eat than the Israelites who whined for cucumbers and onions. As Paul put it in 1 Corinthians 10:13, "No testing has overtaken you that is not common to everyone. God is faithful, and he will not let you be tested beyond your strength, but with the testing will also provide the way out so that you may be able to endure it."

The university campus can be a desert for some students. The familiar and comfortable are gone; the old activities or subjects in which they excelled no longer hold the same excitement; the childhood faith, appropriate to junior high or high school, unchallenged and untested, no longer seems adequate. It may be time to face the first death of a peer or close relative. A long time relationship ends. It's a desert.

The message of scripture is that this is a risky time and a time full of promise. You can squander your time, whining about the old days, questioning the leaders that God places before you, ignoring the manna and quail. But then again, you can draw into a closer relationship with God, you can experience the marvelous guidance of the Holy Spirit, and you can test what it means to really live by the Word of God.

The Christian Journey IV: The Pool

Psalm 114; Ezekiel 47:1-12; Acts 1:1-9; John 4:1-30

We have been thinking about the Christian Journey in terms of some biblical images for the past few weeks. The first image was the path. We saw that one of the earliest — perhaps *the* earliest — designation used to describe those who were devoted to Jesus was "followers of the way," in Greek *hodos*, a path, a road, a highway, but a term that soon enough came to mean a way of life. This image reminds us that commitment to Jesus Christ presupposes that we live in a world where there are a variety of paths we can take, a world where it is not only possible to get lost in a variety of ways, but that it is likely that we will. And it underlines the fact that in Jesus we find a way of life that will enable us to make our way through this world. Christian discipleship is not an abstract philosophy or a code of beliefs: to be a Christian is to live in a certain way, to follow a certain *hodos*, a path.

We thought about the mountain, so often associated with the awesome power of nature and God, the place of the giving of the law, the sermon on the mount, the emotional high of mountaintop experiences. But we noted two other things of which the image of ascending the mounting reminds us: first that Christian discipleship takes effort, foresight, and (as the word indicates) discipline, like that exercised by a skilled mountain climber; and second that we should never be content to stay where we are in our relationship with God, but should constantly be striving for a higher level, what John Wesley referred to as "going on to perfection." This is a point that the apostle Paul frequently made by using athletic metaphors:

> *... forgetting what lies behind and straining forward to what lies ahead, I press on toward the goal for the prize of the heavenly call of God in Christ Jesus.*
> — Philippians 3:14

> *Athletes exercise self-control in all things; they do it to receive a perishable wreath, but we an imperishable one. So I do not run aimlessly, nor do I box as though beating the air.* — 1 Corinthians 9:25-26

Last week we thought of the desert, that inhospitable, arid, unproductive region where so many of the Bible stories take place. As we thought of these stories — the Israelites wandering for forty years, Jesus fasting for forty days, Paul spending time alone in Arabia after his conversion — we saw how that inhospitable, difficult place of temptation was the undoing of some and the proving ground for others. Many of the Israelites stumbled and fell; but for some it was a time of special communion with God, of receiving and meditating on the law, of trusting God for everything.

Circumstances may try us, but we, by God's grace, determine our response. Those who were nourished in the wilderness had no more manna to eat than the Israelites who whined for cucumbers and onions. As Paul put it in 1 Corinthians 10:13: "No testing has overtaken you that is not common to everyone. God is faithful, and he will not let you be tested beyond your strength, but with the testing he will also provide the way out so that you may be able to endure it."

Today's image comes from that testing experience in the wilderness.

> *Tremble, O earth, at the presence of the Lord, at the presence of the God of Jacob, who turns the rock into a pool of water, the flint into a spring of water.*
> — Psalm 114:7-8

Of course, water is needed for our journey no matter what metaphor we use: following Jesus along the way, striving to climb the mountain, facing temptation and fear head-on in the desert. We all know that we can go without food for quite a while, but without adequate water we are soon in dire trouble. But the psalm promises that God provides a spring and a pool to meet our needs: a *spring*, a constant source of nurture and refreshment, and a *pool*, a reservoir of love and grace that our needs will not exhaust.

In his vision of the new age to come, the prophet Ezekiel saw abundant water as a sign of renewal, and new life, a theme which is most familiar to us as Christians in Jesus' familiar encounter with the Samaritan woman at Jacob's well. You will remember how in that story the woman, who had come as women in so much of the world still do, to perform the odious task of drawing the day's water, had understandable difficulty comprehending what Jesus was getting at. "... those who drink of the water that I will give them will never be thirsty. The water that I will give will become in them a spring of water gushing up to eternal life" (John 4:14). "What in the world are you talking about?" was the woman's natural response, but you know the happy ending to the story when she recognized Jesus as the messiah and went out to tell others.

That woman's understandable confusion may be the greatest single danger to first world Christians today. We are so preoccupied with our material world and the marvelous things it can provide, the comforts it can offer, that we have legitimate and understandable trouble getting beyond the notion that there is anything else, or at least anything else that really matters. One of the things that often amazes students and others on international mission trips is the vibrant faith of Christians in the third world. Living in what are unquestionably appalling circumstances, it becomes clear that both because of and in spite of their poverty, these individuals have sought the nurture that comes only from that well-spring of living water, Jesus Christ. This is not at all to glorify poverty, but to underscore the hazards of affluence.

Not long ago I spoke with a former student who had experienced frustration serving a local church after which many clergy would lust: a prestigious church where, most of the time at least, money seemed to be no problem. The frustration came about because the members of that church — at least in this clergy person's estimation — were so self-satisfied that they were not interested in doing anything: growing numerically or in outreach to the area, offering real spiritual nurture or challenge. It was because, my friend said, "the members of that church don't think they need anything." In fact, they may have been dying of thirst. The rock may be beautiful and the flint impressively hard, but they do not provide the water we need. "Tremble, O earth, at the presence of the Lord ... who turns the rock into a pool of water ..." (Psalm 114:7-8).

The pool of water is also a symbol of the response of the Samaritan woman and the resurrected Jesus' commission to the disciples. It is the time-honored metaphor of throwing a pebble into a still pond and watching the rings expand to the very perimeter. The woman has been sufficiently changed that she goes out with a simple proclamation, "Come and see a man who told me everything I have ever done!" And the people went to see. Jesus' final words to the disciples spoke of this same kind of going out: "But you will receive power when the Holy Spirit has come upon you; and you will be my witnesses in Jerusalem, in all Judea and Samaria, and to the ends of the earth." This image of the expanding circles, of a life and faith that constantly become larger and more encompassing (Jerusalem, Judea, Samaria), is an absolutely essential part of our spiritual journey, but one which is easy to overlook for at least two reasons.

On the one hand there is the tendency, particularly prevalent in the academy, to see the Bible in general and Christianity in particular as the source of everything that is selfish, repressive, divisive, mean-spirited, and violent — anything but outreaching and inclusive. In *The Curse of Cain: The Violent Legacy of Monotheism* (University of Chicago Press) Regina Schwartz argues that "the Bible sets up a way of thinking about identity as us versus them." According to her, "The dark side of monotheism is this demand of intolerance..." (quoted in the *Chronicle of Higher Education*, July 3, 1997, A15). Not surprisingly, she sees the self-righteous slaughter in Bosnia, Northern Ireland, and Israel are directly traceable to the Bible. While the book has gotten a lot of attention and praise, the reviewer for *The New Republic* (Peter Berkowitz of Harvard University) accused Dr. Schwartz of "a recklessly one-dimensional reading of the Bible." In my opinion he is correct, and points to a whole variety of ways in which the Bible is read in one-dimensional ways, namely ways that justify me, my opinion, and my group.

One of the most troubling dimensions of our May (1997) Mission Trip to South Africa was coming to grips with how much of the Christian Church supported apartheid in the bad old days — either by acquiescing in silence or actually actively supporting the racist regime often citing isolated Bible passages. They forgot that the first person to proclaim Jesus publicly after the miracle at Cana was a hated Samaritan — and a woman at that! And because of her other Samaritans "... left the city and were on their way to him." The circle was expanding and including.

On the other hand, the whole religious scene today has been deeply influenced by a variety of narrowly egocentric utilitarian New Age spiritualities in which religious practice is seen of use only in terms of its short-term benefit to me. I will adopt this or that "spiritual" practice because it will lower my cholesterol, heighten my on-the-job concentration, or help me lose weight. God does not provide us with pools of water in the desert so that we may all the better worship false gods and sin. Our reaction to these ideas of spirituality should be the same incredulity we would have if we threw that pebble in the pool and saw it swallowed up with no visible effect on the surface of the water: something is seriously wrong — that's just not what's supposed to happen! God provides us with pools and springs of water so that we may better love and serve God and our fellow people, further progress on the way as we follow Jesus, spread out like the rings in the pool.

Karl Rahner, the great twentieth century Canadian theologian, once described the spiritual as that dimension which God has provided that enables us to transcend or break out beyond ourselves and the limits of self-isolation, self-preoccupation, and self-absorption. Is this not just another way of reminding that we are called to "love the Lord your God with all your heart, and with all your soul, and with all your mind, and with all your strength" and, "You shall love your neighbor as yourself" (Mark 12:30-31), another way of saying that as we follow Jesus in the way that leads to the abundant life we are not content to stay where we are and hoard what we have, but are compelled to go out to the ends of the earth?

Fools For The Sake Of Christ

1 Corinthians 4:8-13

April 9, 1996, Supreme Court Justice Antonin Scalia delivered an address in Mississippi on religion and public life, a topic which has gotten a lot of attention the past few years, particularly since the publication of Stephen L. Carter's book *The Culture of Disbelief.* In the course of that speech Justice Scalia quoted from the apostle Paul's letter to the Corinthians where he says that we Christians are sometimes called to be "fools for Christ's sake" or, in the NRSV, "fools for the sake of Christ."

Working from secondhand wire-service reports and without the benefit of a full text of his speech, *Washington Post* reporter Joan Biskupic quoted Scalia and, obviously not recognizing the biblical citation, ventured the opinion that by this Scalia meant that "the modern world dismisses Christians as fools for holding to their traditional beliefs." I don't know if people were more indignant with the fact that a U.S. Supreme Court Justice would allude to religious faith, or that he seemed to imply an anti-religious cultural bias, but that phrase set off one of those tempests within the beltway teapot. For the next ten days denunciations appeared in the pages of *The Washington Post, The New York Times* and letters to *The Christian Century* as well as, I am sure, lots of other sources that I never peruse.

Now, I will confess that I have never been a member of the Justice Scalia fan club, and I am sure that many of those piling on were taking advantage of the moment because of past skirmishes and disagreements with him as well as his increasingly bitter rhetoric. Indeed, as one of the justice's former law clerks remarked, "If Scalia were to announce that the world was round, the Flat Earth Society would be flooded with applications from law school professors and National Public Radio would soon broadcast a series entitled 'The Shape of the World Reconsidered.'" But what really caught my attention, as a minister and sometime professor of the Bible, is that nobody — no reporter, no researcher, no data bank — caught the fact that Scalia was quoting that venerable book that adorns our coffee tables. It was only after ten days of flap that Robert A. Sirico, an attorney who also happens to be a Catholic priest, pointed out in *The Wall Street Journal* what should have been obvious, that Scalia was quoting the apostle Paul. And in good priestly fashion he gave a little biblical interpretation:

> *Saint Paul's remark about himself and the other apostles being "fools for Christ's sake" was meant to draw the contrast with the haughty and self-satisfied. It was a remark born of humility when faced with God's power over our lives.*

There are two things that jump out of this episode at me — maybe really two sides of the same coin. *The first is the increasing, and increasingly bemoaned, ignorance of Scripture on the part of all of us, inside as well as outside the church.* I was recently speaking with a chaplain friend who had been accosted by the Art History professor at his university. His colleague was complaining that in his courses on medieval and Renaissance art he was reduced to *telling Bible stories* because none of the students recognized the scenes portrayed in painting, sculpture, and stained glass. "Can you imagine," this professor bellowed, "that I have to spend my time telling students about Abraham's willingness to sacrifice Isaac, the crossing of the Red Sea, even the Annunciation!" The chaplain found it somewhat amusing and responded that there were worse things in life than telling Bible stories, and of course there are plenty of worse things. But the episode of Justice Scalia's speech reminds us that this lack of familiarity with a text which is not only regarded as sacred by Christians and Jews but which has provided a *lingua franca* of stories, images, and phrases for Western Civilization *really does matter*. It does not always just amount to a bemused professor having to divert from her or his syllabus to fill in the blanks. It often means that we have profound yet unrecognized cultural, religious, and political disagreements about who we are, the nature of the world, and the importance of our individual and corporate decisions — topics that the Bible addresses directly and repeatedly. Because of this ignorance, while thinking we are in dialogue, and assuming a common moral and religious base, we are really speaking past one another.

In his 1995 book *Cease Fire: Searching for Sanity in America's Culture Wars,* evangelical author Tom Sine does an analysis of how he believes Christians of every variety and theology have been co-opted by non-biblical world-views. He points out, for example, how many progressive mainline Protestants and Roman Catholics have committed themselves to working for a positive future. They have embraced such biblical mandates as care for the environment as an aspect of our call to be good stewards of God's creation, efforts to ensure justice and peace for all persons, and the affirmation and utilization of the gifts of all members of the Christian church, not overlooking women, ethnic minorities, and the disabled.

But he also shows how some of these progressive Christians have overlooked or ignored the biblical contention that we are all sinners in need of God's grace. This, he contends, is because many progressive Christians have, perhaps unconsciously, bought into the popular notion of victimization. How comforting it is to feel that all of *my* problems are due to the fact that I am being victimized by big business, the press, the government, you name it. *I* am not in need of any kind of salvation or redemption, because nothing is wrong with *me.* The problem is with all my victimizers. They need to change, be regulated more closely, be thrown out of office, and get off my back. So, Sine contends, while getting many biblical teachings right, many progressive Christians overlook the Bible's overarching theme that we all need to look within ourselves in the light of God's love, and acknowledge our own sin and need for redemption.

On the other hand, Sine asks, "How is it possible, that the political agenda of the religious right looks so much like that of the secular right, when the leaders of the religious right contend that their views come directly from the Bible? Either the secular right has been divinely inspired all along and no one noticed or the religious right has allowed their agenda for social change to be determined by right-wing political ideology instead of Scripture ... I believe conservative Protestants have been co-opted."

I think he is right about how many of us Christians — right-wing, left-wing, liberal, conservative, Catholic, Protestant — are increasingly basing our theologies and opinions not on Scripture and the tradition of the Church, but on other popular world-views and ideologies without even realizing it, largely because of our profound lack of familiarity with the broad sweep of Scripture and its inescapable themes.

I recently read the review of a book on management (Knoke, William, *Bold New World*, Kodansha International, NYC) which celebrated the fact that as a result of computers, cellular phones, modems and modern communication and transportation we are now in the age of knowing "everything everywhere." As many of us find ourselves on the on-ramp to the information superhighway we probably need to be reminded that having access to all kinds of information is not the same as knowing, understanding, and using it properly. And this is, of course, an age-old problem in new clothes. "Already you have all you want! Already you have become rich!" the apostle Paul wrote to some Corinthian Christians. They were rich, wise, and strong, held in honor in their own opinion — or as my mother would say they "thought they knew it all" — while in their eyes Paul and the other apostles were weak and held in disrepute — "fools for the sake of Christ."

And this brings me to the second thing, or the other side of the coin. *Authentic biblical faith, based as it is on a personal encounter with God and a recreation of the self in the divine image, will always be out of step with the pragmatic way that things are done in "the real world." It will always appear "foolish."* "Has not God made foolish the wisdom of the world?" Paul asked in the introduction to his letters to the contentious congregation at Corinth. The gospel message of Jesus turns things upside down, saying that forgiveness is better than vindictiveness, that peace is of more value than strife, that we should give rather than receive. And we tend to notice people who are standing on their heads. So Paul knew that he looked like a fool. "When reviled, we bless; when persecuted we endure; when slandered, we speak kindly."

Some of you no doubt saw a story on *20/20* about the youth minister who was dismissed from his church position when his child was discovered to have AIDS. The story focused on the effect the dismissal had on both the father and the grandfather of the boy, both of whom were Southern Baptist pastors, the grandfather having served for a time as "head" of the convention. Two things struck me. First, the expected bitterness of the young clergyman at his abrupt dismissal. He, like many of us no doubt, felt that in their pragmatism that congregation missed a chance to show the community what it really means to follow Jesus. But more inspiring was the story of the grandfather who, rather than enjoying his well-deserved retirement, has mounted a one-man crusade, preaching and speaking wherever he can, often in remote, rural congregations, telling them of the love of Christ, and how that love should be extended to HIV positive persons. In some ways this distinguished elder of the church looks foolish traipsing around the hinterlands, and that's the point, isn't it?

You don't need national television for that kind of story. A seminary classmate of mine became quite concerned about AIDS — and in particular the church's rejection of HIV positive persons — after a life-long friend was infected by the virus. The congregation he served made it clear that they did not appreciate his activism on behalf of AIDS education. He ended up taking early retirement. I know many people thought he was playing the fool. And for that matter, how many persons who spend their lives in the mission field or the classroom or on the small campus or in a modest pulpit or simply living largely unnoticed lives of faithfulness and service are motivated not, as many assume, by a shortage of talent or by a lack of ambition, but by a desire to follow Jesus Christ. There are, after all, things that money and position can't buy; and, as incredible as it may seem to say today, there still are times when "what's in it for me?" is the wrong question. Nobody wants to look foolish or be thought the fool. But as Justice Scalia noted, that's exactly what the gospel sometimes calls us to do.

It is no accident that in many of the world's great cathedrals in addition to the vaults and spires, the buttresses and wonderful stained glass windows, there are gargoyles, grinning foolishly down at all they see. There are times when we all need to take ourselves less seriously and be willing to stand on our heads. There are times when we need to open ourselves up to the love and grace of God regardless of the kind of spectacle it may make us or how at odds it may place us with prevailing ideologies. Sometimes each of us needs to be a fool for the sake of Christ.

Eighteen Years Is Long Enough

Jeremiah 1:4-10; Luke 13:10-17

A few weeks ago the officers of Kappa Chi, our co-ed Christian service fraternity, had a planning retreat in a small town just east of Indianapolis. We took our Saturday afternoon Burger King and Taco Bell to a picturesque park where I spotted a little boy who looked to be about five years old. He was the spitting image of my son Tim as he looked eighteen years ago when he was five. A lot of water has passed over the dam in those years: Tim had grown a great deal and now towers over me. He is a cook at a local restaurant, so if you go there and have a good meal, tell me about it. For me sometimes, a day in the park with little Timmy in some ways seems like only yesterday, but I know it's really been a long time — long enough for him to grow into an independent adult. My guess is that as a lot of you, especially the freshmen, suffered through plenty of similar reminiscing from your parents as you got ready to come to college.

The Old Testament story of the commissioning of Jeremiah as a prophet does not say that he was eighteen years old, but it doesn't seem unreasonable to assume that that was about his age, that of a young man. Like many of the great prophets — Moses, Isaiah, Ezekiel — Jeremiah objects that he is unqualified for the awesome task of being appointed a "prophet to the nations" to speak for God. We generally assume that these objections were not just lame excuses, but genuine expressions of a sense of inadequacy, just not being up to the task.

Jeremiah's objection that he does not know how to speak because he is too young and inexperienced is certainly not an unreasonable reservation. The Judeo-Christian tradition, after all, is one that has a content. It is not just a matter of personal opinion or feeling: we are a "people of the book," the Bible. And as such, the

Judeo-Christian tradition is by nature conservative, which is simply to say that we conserve and pass along that tradition of the book. "For I received from the Lord what I also handed on to you," Paul wrote the Corinthians in words we often quote in Communion services, but which in a larger sense summarize how we pass the faith along from generation to generation. Because we believe the Bible to be inspired by God, we find it to be continually inspiring in new and often surprising ways, but we are, by definition, connected to this tradition.

Jeremiah knew that he was not an elder of the community, not a gray head, and so because of his youth, he felt unqualified to speak on behalf of the God of his fathers. This can be a good thing. Knowing the limitations imposed by one's own inexperience, knowing what you don't know, are valid reasons for not recklessly biting off more than you can chew.

But there are three things in God's commission that more than canceled out Jeremiah's youth and inexperience. First, God said that God had been working in Jeremiah's life since before his birth in ways of which Jeremiah was unaware. This notion, that God is at work in our lives in unnoticed ways, preparing us for unexpected things, is a key teaching of scripture. (Theologians call this prevenient grace.) It is one of the reasons that spiritual discernment is such an important gift in the Christian community. Sometimes what God is doing in our lives is more obvious to others than it is to us! Second, God touched Jeremiah and empowered him in a particular way for the ministry to which he was being called. "Now I have put my words in your mouth." Jeremiah was right — he *wasn't* prepared, but God could prepare him. Finally, and most crucially, the particular task to which God was calling Jeremiah was one for which his youth was a particular asset, not a liability. "To pluck up and to pull down, to destroy and to overthrow, to build and to plant."

As the story of Jeremiah's public ministry unfolds two things become clear: the nation was facing new challenges for which old solutions were inadequate; and many people were putting the wrong kind of emphasis on the truth they had received from previous generations. Many Israelites erroneously believed that because they were God's chosen people they could do no wrong, and that God would bless and preserve their nation no matter what. Many had an almost magical view of the externals of their faith and believed that as long as ritual sacrifice was taking place in the Temple the nation would be preserved regardless of the greed, selfishness, exploitation, and hypocrisy of the people. It was misplaced "conservatism" if you will, a hollow traditionalism. Jeremiah had to tear down those false notions in order to replant and rebuild authentic faith. It is said that "Tradition is the living faith of the dead, traditionalism is the dead faith of the living." The task of replacing traditionalism with an appropriate use of tradition is one that is well suited to the young.

I don't know who all of you are yet, but I know that there are individuals in this room who may feel like Jeremiah: that they are too young, too inexperienced, too unschooled in the faith, to do much for God. But I also know that eighteen years is long enough for a lot to happen. God has been at work in your life in particular ways; you have background and experiences and strengths that are yours alone. And I believe that God is calling you to use those gifts in unique and new and different ways on our campus and in our community. Our situation is not identical to Jeremiah's. But there are many needs for ministry and service for which seventeen or eighteen or nineteen years of preparation is plenty of time, especially when God enables your heart or mouth or hands.

This brings us to the other story, the one where eighteen years is specifically mentioned as the time span for which a woman had been crippled by a spirit. There was someone or something that was literally weighing this woman down so that she could not stand up straight. Over the years I have met and talked with enough people who were literally bowed down with guilt, individuals who could not stand up or sit up straight, or look anyone in the eye or sit still to know that this is not just metaphorical or symbolic language. This woman had a spirit, a possession or demon, that for eighteen years had ruined her life, had kept her from being the person God had created her to be.

Once again, I don't know who they are, but from statistics alone, I know that we have such persons in the entering freshman class. It used to be that when students went off to the university parents worried that they might have their first beer or their first sexual adventure. Those are still, of course, valid concerns. But I now regularly talk with students who have packed a lot into their eighteen years. They have done a lot more than experiment with beer, and arrive on campus as recovering addicts. Or perhaps they have been the caretaker in a co-dependent family and are driven to meet everyone else's needs while totally ignoring their own. They have been the victims of abuse or incest or rape; they have had abortions or had children or been responsible for someone's pregnancy. "Do you remember hearing about that kid who was molested by the minister or the teacher or the coach?" somebody will ask. I'm no longer surprised when they say, "that was my neighbor" or "that was my brother" or "that was me." And the good news of the gospel is that for however long these individuals have had that spirit which weighs them down, it is long enough: eighteen years is long enough, eighteen months is long enough. God's desire is for you to be free of those impediments and to accept the freedom that God gives you to serve God and your fellow human beings.

It is striking in this gospel story that not everyone is overjoyed by this woman's release from her long-time bondage. The synagogue leader's objection is based on a distorted understanding of keeping the Sabbath day holy. But I wonder if there wasn't more at work. He may have known, or suspected, what spirit was binding this woman and felt that it was appropriate for her to be stooped over, to be prevented from living a full life. She had it coming because of who she was or where she was from or something she had done! Many of the persons who have presented the kind of situations I mentioned a moment ago have gone to a parent or a counselor or a minister only to be told, in effect, "It must be your own fault; you've gotten yourself into this drama, now you play it out." In the face of such insensitivity, Jesus Christ still says, "Ought not this person, bound for so long, be set free from this bondage?"

Eighteen years is plenty long enough. It is long enough to be shaped and molded and equipped by God for specific tasks of ministry and service. And it is long enough to be crippled, to be bent over by events and spirits that would hold us captive. Sometimes these two go hand in hand, and the individual who has experienced God's grace and healing is the best one to reach out to others who are hurting.

As we begin this new academic year, let's use this time of worship to say that eighteen years is long enough. For some it is time to be freed from the past; for some it is time to put the past to work for God and others; for some it is time for both.

Meeting Jesus At The Well

John 4:5-30, 39-42

The familiar story of Jesus' encounter with the Samaritan woman at Jacob's well is loaded with meaning. It is a pattern for considering our meetings with Jesus at various times in our lives.

The story begins with Jesus asking this woman to perform a simple task, well within her ability: to get him a drink from the well. She did, after all, have the equipment. But she didn't want to do it and was able to provide some good reasons why she shouldn't. Every day of our lives, Jesus Christ asks us to do specific simple things which are as well within our ability as drawing a drink of water was for that woman: to speak a word of witness or share an act of kindness; to spend some time with a distressed or confused classmate; to tutor at the Power Program or help with the Adopt-a-Class Program; to have an adopted grandparent, write a letter or go on a Habitat work day. These are not big dramatic things, but little every day manageable tasks that Jesus asks of us; tasks that are well within our ability, just like drawing that drink of water from the well.

Like the woman, of course, we may choose to respond negatively to such requests, and always with good reason. "I would have liked to have spent some time with that student whose father died, but I had to study for a test. I'm not so sure about that service project; I once knew someone who volunteered at a soup kitchen, and he had a bad experience — I think he got robbed. I thought about taking part in that program, but I heard that there were some Lutherans in the group — or maybe they were Baptists or Presbyterians or something — whatever, they were some people that I don't like." "How is it that you, a Jew, ask a drink of me, a woman of Samaria?" There are always some good reasons why we should respond negatively. When Jesus asks us to do something for him, we are being asked to relinquish a certain amount of control and to take a certain risk, and none of us likes to lose control and take risks.

In the past fifteen to twenty years, many churches have been designed in response to consumer surveys. In several midwestern suburban areas the surveys have had similar results. People want the church to provide a good community center with an excellent gym and Nautilus-caliber training equipment; they want quality affordable day care and after school care for children; they want a variety of self-help and support groups; and they want sermons dealing with timely issues like money management and enhancing self-esteem. What they do not want are worship services where they are asked to participate or sing hymns; and they do not want sermons dealing with topics like sin, personal ethics, world hunger, or self-sacrifice. In response to such trends, within the past few years one of the larger churches in Evansville discontinued serving communion or baptizing people during regular worship services. They have discovered that people don't want religious rituals that talk about the new birth or the body and blood of Christ; they want a fellowship that will basically affirm who they are as good and worthwhile individuals and encourage them to maximize their potential. After watching a fairly detailed television account of one of these rapidly growing churches a few years ago, my daughter remarked that it was good for the planners to ask what people want out of a church, but that it might not hurt also to ask what God wants out of the church. There is the control issue again. Does God have any control over the church, or is the church simply an institution designed to meet the articulated desires of its members? The woman at the well felt comfortable turning Jesus down. Sometimes we do too.

Now, someone may be thinking, in fairness to that woman we have to acknowledge that she had almost no chance of understanding what Jesus was talking about. With the benefit of hindsight, we know that Jesus was speaking about "living water" symbolically, meaning a source of constant spiritual refreshment. But this phrase, "living water," was more commonly used to mean fresh running water from a spring or river as opposed to water standing in a cistern or a well. The woman naturally enough assumed that this was what Jesus was speaking about, a source of constant fresh running water. That initial misunderstanding made it all but impossible for her to comprehend the business about water gushing up inside the individual. We seem to have a mental standoff. This is, of course, one of the conundrums of the Christian life: Jesus calls us to have faith and be transformed, but until we have some faith we may not see any need or possibility for transformation.

Something often happens when students go on a mission or service trip. Afterward, they will frequently share that they were not stupid or insensitive before the trip: they always knew that there were hungry, poor, and homeless people. But until they went to D. C. or St. Louis or Cleveland or Denver or wherever, they didn't *really* know about homeless and hungry people and how the church can help them. And once they *really* know, they see dimensions of poverty in Evansville or in their home communities of which they were simply unaware before. If they had never taken the risk, they would not have grown in their understanding of the needs of people, how God is working to meet those needs, and what role *they* can play in making God's will a reality for others. Jesus calls us to have faith and be transformed; but until we step out on faith we may not ever see the need for transformation.

The story moves on to this business of the five previous husbands and the man with whom the woman is now living. Again the issue is control. How much does this woman control what Jesus knows about her? The embarrassing answer is "not much." While an important aspect of this story is clearly Jesus' prophetic powers, it is also a reminder that things are often not as big a secret as we might wish. Some years ago I worked at a very small school where one of the professors had become not just an alcoholic, but a first-class drunk. He would show up for class so inebriated that he was incoherent; he would sit behind his desk and fall into a stupored sleep; or he would just miss classes. One day I confronted him about his problem drinking. He was absolutely thunder struck — you would have thought that I had the most astounding second-sight since biblical times. He was really convinced that his drinking was totally under control and not noticeable. As you are well aware, co-dependent families are often pulled into a cycle of attempting to hold things together and patch things up so that nobody will notice what's going on, when the situation is all too painfully obvious.

Students who are experiencing academic difficulty or are not adjusting well to campus life are sometimes astounded, sometimes offended, that someone — a professor, a resident assistant, the chaplain — expresses a concern about how they're doing. "You've been talking with my parents!" they might say. "My roommate has betrayed secrets I told her in confidence." No, not at all. It is just that things may be more obviously wrong than you guess. Much neurosis and psychosis is the result of trying to bury things in our subconscious, trying to keep things secret even from ourselves; but we can't do it. We can wear masks and fool a lot of people for a long time. We can even fool ourselves for a while, but the charade cannot last forever. "Nothing is hidden," Jesus says in Luke 8, "that will not be made known." At its most basic level, this means that we cannot control what other people know about us to the extent that we may wish; and *nothing* is hidden from God.

It makes us uncomfortable when the spotlight suddenly turns on us and we naturally enough want to divert its glare. "I've always wondered about this Mount Gerizim business," the woman suddenly says. "Why is it that we Samaritans worship there while you Jews worship in Jerusalem?" It is amazing how often religious issues are used to avoid spiritual matters. Every minister can tell stories of getting on a plane or train and striking up a friendly and relaxed conversation that grinds to a halt when the business of one's vocation comes up. "I'm a United Methodist minister" leads to a stunned and stony silence. Then, after a long pause, some response: "Well, you know, I've always wondered why the Baptists throw people in a tub," or "What about those Jehovah's Witnesses?" or "What is it with Catholic priests and little kids?" Like the woman at the well, there is an immediate attempt to divert attention to some "religious" issue, lest the follow-up question be something like, "Have you prayed to God lately?" or "Do you know the meaning of 'adultery'?" No, we don't want to get into that kind of personal thing. And as those who design churches by consumer poll remind us, people very much control institutional religion. There are individuals who are very out of touch with their inner spiritual self and who are very afraid of self-disclosure who are really up on church structure and polity, or on the shortcomings of every denomination. If the topic of God or religion ever comes up they can fill the space with verbiage without ever getting close to their spiritual self.

In situations like this, it is tempting to say, "None of that matters. Baptism doesn't matter; what hymns you sing, what church you attend don't matter." But they *do* matter. Jesus reminded the woman who had her sudden interest in the proper place to worship that salvation was from the Jews and that the Jerusalem temple was the proper place to offer sacrifice. These issues are important. But he went on. "God is spirit, and those who worship God must worship in spirit and truth." The form of worship, the place of worship, the type of worship are all important as means to the end that we worship God in spirit and truth. There is always a problem when we become so preoccupied with the means, we never get around to the end.

This has been kind of a rough conversation so far. Jesus has not allowed us to "just say no" to serving him by doing everyday, manageable things; he has reminded us that we don't control things as tightly as we might think and that things aren't as secret as we may imagine; and now we discover that we can't escape personal scrutiny by talking about the church bureaucracy or the fight the congregation is having over what color the new carpet should be. No, Jesus demands that we look deeply inside ourselves and that we look squarely at him and make some response.

The woman is still there. She could have gotten up and walked away. The Samaritans and Jews didn't get along very well, so nobody would have given a second thought to that. But she stayed. In spite of the misunderstanding over what "living water" meant, in spite of her obvious discomfort over her personal life coming to light, she stayed. We always have the option of checking out of our conversation with Jesus, and lots of us do. As soon as someone says something we don't like, our response is, "That's not for me! I'll find a church where they don't talk about this stuff!" If things get a little too personal, if it looks like we might not be totally in control, we check out.

The woman stays. She has the same desire we all have to be in touch with God. It may make some demands of us and it may be uncomfortable, but if we can be in touch with God, it will be worth it. As it turns out, she really knew all she needed to know to respond to Jesus: "I know the Messiah is coming." I know that God is working in a special way to make it possible for us to experience more fully God's presence, to be in a special relationship with God. Maybe that's why this woman went through so many bad relationships with men, because she was looking for intimacy. Maybe there were other dark secrets that she was scared to death Jesus was going to spill out. But she knew that at some point Messiah would come, and Jesus said, "I am he." She knew enough to keep the dialogue going. And off she went, leaving her water jar behind.

We all know enough to keep the dialogue going. You know that God loves all humankind, which God created. You know how over the long course of history God has worked for the salvation of persons. You know that in the fullness of time Jesus came as the full embodiment of God's love, a love that was willing to go to the cross. And you know that Christ speaks to us today just as he did to that woman long ago. The only question for us is, "Will we keep the dialogue going?" Will we respond positively to Jesus' requests of us, will we take risks and step out on faith, or will we get up and say, "I don't feel like doing that." Will we be able to accept that God sees us as we really are, not the masks we wear or the public persona we present? Will we stay with the conversation to the end? Whenever we are willing to be challenged by God and to confront the reality of Jesus Christ face to face, we are able to leave one more water jar behind, and go out serving, witnessing, and growing, as Christians.

Something New, Something Old

Matthew 13:31-36a, 44-58; Isaiah 49:1-6

The story is told of an American service man visiting a South Sea island during World War II. His friendly host proudly brought a copy of the Bible out of his hut and said, "This is my most prized possession." With obvious disdain, the GI replied, "Oh, I've outgrown that old stuff!" The islander, whose tribe had recently accepted Christianity and undergone significant changes from their former lifestyle which included cannibalism, responded, "It's a good thing for you it's new to us, or you would have been a meal as soon as we saw you." What is regarded as new or old, relevant or quaintly out of date, really does make a difference sometimes.

This was a theme that was particularly important to the writer of the Gospel of Matthew. As a devout Jew who had come to accept Jesus as Messiah, one of this evangelist's special themes was to show the way in which Jesus fulfilled all the old expectations in a new and often unexpected way. Over and over Matthew, and Matthew alone, explicitly points out how Jesus' words and deeds "fulfilled what was foretold by the prophets." Jesus was, after all, not exactly the sort of Messiah many persons expected. They were looking for a new king like David, a military leader who would throw out the Roman occupation army and set up a Jewish state. Instead, Jesus came as the Suffering Servant of whom the prophet Isaiah had spoken, an idea of messiahship which had not caught the popular imagination.

One day after giving a whole series of parables, and explaining only one (the Parable of the Sower), Jesus asked his disciples if they understood all this. "Yes," they answered (I have a feeling somewhat haltingly and feebly) and then Jesus told them,

> *"Therefore every scribe who has been trained for the kingdom of heaven is like the master of a household who brings out of his treasure what is new and what is old."*

Three things jump out at us. First, that in this little saying, we seem to find Matthew's life-mission spelled out, which may be why he alone records these words of Jesus. Second, this is the only place in any Gospel that Jesus uses the term "scribe" as a figure for those who would follow him. The scribes, of course, were those trained in copying and interpreting the Jewish law, who were devoted to applying the old law to new situations. So being a disciple of Jesus requires close attention to detail. And third, the word order Jesus uses jumps out at us as much today and it would have twenty centuries ago. We expect to hear about the old and the new, "Something old, something new, something borrowed, something blue." Particularly in religious circles, which are inherently conservative and always building upon the tradition of the past, we expect to hear it that way. But Jesus, surely deliberately, says that the scribe trained for the kingdom of God brings out that which is new and that which is old.

At the beginning of a new academic year, this text highlights three of the great themes of scripture for all of us, and especially for those who are new to the University of Evansville. (1) This emphasis on the new as well as the old underscores the fundamental theme of all Jesus' public preaching: that the kingdom of God was breaking into the world in a new and exciting way in his ministry and that many things that people had thought about and hoped about and dreamed about for ages were beginning to become reality. The problem was that persons with old expectations and old mindsets would fail to see what was happening. They would still be thinking of the tiny mustard seed or the little lump of dough instead of the firm branches of the tree and the raised loaf.

This is what the Apostle Paul was getting at when he warned that "the letter kills, but the Spirit gives life." We must always live by the Holy Spirit in the now, guided by the past but never held back by it. James Conrad, a Kansas attorney, tells how he once felt anxiety and anger toward clients who failed to pay him, particularly since he was struggling to meet his own expenses. One Christmas he decided it was time to put this behind him and he wrote to those who owed him forgiving their debts. He asked his clients to forgive him if he had offended them and that they would forgive at least one other person who owed them money or who had hurt them. One client called to say he had forgiven a debt of a hundred dollars; another wept in gratitude; a third party paid his bill and referred a new client. But most important, Conrad no longer lived in anger and resentment. Empowered by a spirit of forgiveness, he moved from the old into the new.

Living in the past is a danger for every one of us. Whether it is a romanticized past of the "good old days," the defeatist past of being an outcast at school or the object of ridicule or abuse at home, or a past of unresolved guilt and resentment doesn't matter so much as that it is the past and we are called to live now. What you are is much more important that what you were; and what God is calling you to become is the most important of all.

(2) Because we live in the now, our understanding of ourselves, others, and God must constantly be maturing. Charles H. Duell was Director of the U. S. Patent Office when he declared in 1899 that, "Everything that can be invented has been invented." President Grover Cleveland was stating what many felt was self-evident when he said that "Sensitive and responsible women do not want to vote." Robert Miliken, one of the early Nobel Laureates in physics, assured the world, "There is no likelihood that we can ever tap the power of the atom." Lord Kelvin, President of the Royal Scientific Society, put one matter to rest in 1895 when he said that "Heavier-than-air flying machines are simply impossible." And it was Tris Speaker, himself a former ball player, who observed that "Babe Ruth made a big mistake when he gave up pitching." These anecdotes are amusing because, aside from a good dose of embarrassment, nobody's life was ruined by them. A failure to keep up with change is not always so benign.

It is very predictable that students will come to this university, any university, and "lose their faith." The same thing happens to particular people when they are abused or exploited by a trusted friend or family member, go through a divorce or experience the death of a loved one, or when they first see grinding poverty face to face and cannot comprehend how a loving God could allow such suffering and so determine there must be no God. But why is it that at the very same junctures in life others are strengthened in their faith and transformed? They give their lives to serving others who are going through life's traumas. They are moved to become missionaries or spend time in the Peace Corps. They begin a support group for others suffering the injustice and hurt they have experienced. How is this so?

One reason is that some of these persons, faced with a new dilemma, if I may paraphrase Jesus, "(are) like the master of a household who brings out of his treasure what is ... old." They bring out an immature, childish (not childlike, childish) faith and find it wanting, and so they discard it rather than allow it to mature. Unfortunately, in some circles, including certain academic circles, this discarding of faith is mistaken as a sign of maturation.

In the Sermon on the Mount Jesus tells us, "Unless your righteousness *exceeds* that of the scribes and Pharisees, you will never enter the kingdom of heaven" (Matthew 5:20). The Pharisees, of course, represented the height of religious devotion in Jesus' time; but it was a devotion that was tied to a traditional, legalistic understanding of God's will. So over and over again Jesus cited specific laws, saying "You have heard that it was said to those of ancient times," and then giving a new, higher, and more personal interpretation, "But I say to you." It was not enough to avoid murder, Jesus says, one must not think degrading thoughts about fellow human beings. Not only should one eschew adultery, one must not look at members of the opposite sex with lust, and so on. As our world changes, as we mature, we must constantly strive for a deeper level of personal responsibility and a more profound understanding of the world around us and God's role in that world. We should, in other words, lose our childish faith and replace it with something new.

(3) The third new thing is obvious because we know the end of the Jesus story as well as the beginning and the middle. At the very end of Matthew's telling of the Gospel story, Jesus stands on the

mountaintop and tells the disciples, "Go therefore and make disciples of all nations." This is significant because Matthew was a convert from Judaism writing for Jews. And many of the Jews of that era had become very particularistic, seeing themselves as God's chosen people and more concerned with keeping themselves pure than in reaching out. They had clearly forgotten Isaiah's words about the people of Israel becoming a "light to the nations." So the new/old message that comes out of the householder's treasure is that we must always move from the specific to the general, from the local to the global.

All of us begin in a particular setting: a certain family, a hometown, a local church, a given denomination, a native land. But God so loved the world, and we are called to reach out beyond narrow boundaries. Jesmina grew up in West Germany. Soon after East and West Germany united Jesmina began to resent East Germans and the Eastern Europeans who poured into her homeland by the thousands. Jesmina came to the United States and met Marta, a Czech, one of those Jesmina had come to dislike so intensely. She and Marta quickly became friends, and now both of them were outsiders whose presence was resented by some Americans.

This little vignette reminds us how much our world is like the divided world in which Jesus of Nazareth and the evangelist Matthew lived. Jesus risked his reputation by talking and eating with those who were scorned by others because they were outcasts. We don't have to go to a foreign country to find those who are different; we draw boundaries all the time, often unconsciously separating those who are "insiders" and "outsiders," "winners" and "losers."

Today's Gospel story ends on a cautionary note which serves as a kind of acted parable of Jesus' teaching. The hometown folks are so fixated on who Jesus *had been* that they could not see who he *was*! And the Gospel says, "And he did not do many deeds of power there, because of their unbelief." If we bring out only the old, we can actually thwart God's graceful purposes!

So here you are, bringing lots of old, and I hope most of it "good" old, experiences. But it is always time to bring out that which is new as well to discover what dreams are reality; to discard childish ideas and faith and replace them with more mature thoughts; and to move out into a wider world.

"Ascribe To The Lord The Glory Due His Name ..."

Psalm 96:8

Twenty years ago I was the young minister of children and youth at a large United Methodist church on the east coast. The semi-retired minister of visitation was the Reverend Walter Donoway, who was approaching his ninetieth birthday. He made regular hospital and home rounds and on Sunday mornings often said the prayer or received the offering. He had never been a tall man and was now somewhat stooped. But when it came time for the offering he stood erect. Unlike most ministers I've heard, he didn't talk about the pledge drive nor encourage us to be cheerful givers. Instead he would intone in a firm voice, "Ascribe to the Lord the glory of his name! Bring an offering, and come into the courts of the Lord. Worship the Lord in holy splendor!" (Psalm 96:8-9). It was a striking thing.

These words of the Psalmist, like old Reverend Donoway, may strike many modern persons as old-fashioned and quaint. The idea of ascribing anything to God, let alone glory, whatever that means, is not very in tune with the times. And yet as odd and quaint as it may sound, this concept lies at the very heart of what all worship is supposed to be, according to the Bible.

As twentieth century people we are not given much to praise. We are more likely to be cynical or critical than we are to be found praising someone. We expect people to complain about how they were ripped off or taken advantage of, of how they always get the short end of the stick. Rodney Dangerfield made a career out of lack of respect. In fact, if someone does begin to praise a product or a service we become suspicious and wonder if he is on the take.

Praise is not a normal part of our lives, so it may not be a natural part of our approach to God either.

The English word "worship" comes from the Saxon "worthship" — acknowledging that which is worthy of our praise and attention. In the Bible, worship is homage. It is the attitude and activity designed to recognize and describe the worth of the person or thing who is the focus of the worship. A variety of Hebrew and Greek words that might literally be rendered "to serve," "to adore," to "fall-down," or "to prostrate one's self" are all translated into English as "worship." Worship, then, is reverence, centering life on something or someone whom we deem worthy of our adoration. It is, in other words, "ascribing to the Lord the glory due his name!"

If we stop to think about all this it is no surprise that much of what goes on in modern churches and religious groups, including what we often call "worship," is not worship in the biblical sense, but something else which may, in fact, be quite useful. A lot of religious instruction goes on. Bible study groups, retreats, sermons and religious addresses on moral and theological issues, and motivational talks are all very important. The Christian faith has a content and we need to remind ourselves constantly of what that content is. Our Lord calls us to take up our cross daily and follow him, and we may need help and encouragement in discerning how best to follow him faithfully. So religious instruction is necessary for true worship, to having God at the center of our attention and the focus of our lives. But the trouble with content-oriented instruction is that it may simply be regarded as "interesting ideas," "one opinion among many" to be acted upon or ignored depending on how we feel. I've counseled with enough young adults who said that they absolutely did not believe in pre-marital sex who were now dealing with an unwanted pregnancy to be fully aware of this!

We all like to be entertained and to feel good. The religious entertainment business is a multi-billion dollar industry. Obviously religiously-oriented entertainment is preferred to filthy humor or obscene movies. Like instruction, religious entertainment may or may not lead to real worship. This is, of course, a criticism often aimed at music and other arts in public worship. Whether a Bach motet or a medley of praise choruses, a humorous skit or a deeply moving drama, the charge is often made that it is "just entertainment" aimed at an assembly of people and not worship of God. And I need say little about the fact that many churches end up being personality cults in which the minister, his opinions, her experiences or problems or family become the real focus rather than God.

The challenge is always to have instruction, music, and other arts and the personality of the worship leaders point toward God rather than themselves. Søren Kierkegaard, the nineteenth century Danish philosopher and theologian, gave a useful analogy. Many people attend church thinking of themselves as the audience, he wrote, and regarding the minister, the choir, and others leading in worship as actors in a drama. The audience is then free to critique the "performance" of those in worship. But, said Kierkegaard, they have it all backwards. In reality, the minister and other worship leaders are not the actors, but functioning more like the director and prompters in a stage play. The real actors are those in the congregation who come not to watch, but to worship God. Their efforts are not directed toward each other nor toward the minister and choir, but toward God who is the real audience. God is the one who observes our every action and knows our every thought, and worship is the time when we really focus our attention on that fact. The fundamental purpose of worship, then, is not to please, entertain or even instruct us, although all these things may be useful byproducts; the fundamental purpose of worship is to focus totally on God.

Psalm 96, which was probably sung at the annual New Year's festival in Jerusalem, links together two great aspects of worship. It is a hymn in three verses. The short middle verse that Reverend Donoway used to quote is the exhortation to worship. The first verse tells us that we worship God because of who God is. God is the creator; Yahweh is the only real God. All other loyalties that seem so important are really idolatrous. God is the source of salvation in Jesus Christ.

But while the first verse tells us that we worship God because of who God is, the third says that when we worship God we are reminded of who we are. We are reminded that we are God's creatures, here with a purpose, and with certain limitations. "Say among the nations, 'The Lord reigns! ... God will judge the world with righteousness and the peoples with truth.' " Because God created us, because God sent God's son to die for us, because God cares about us, worship that focuses on God cannot help but have an effect on us.

This is why real worship — not just talk about religious ideas, or religious entertainment, or a religious personality cult — but real worship, is so crucial for us. We have mastered many aspects of our environment. We have conquered the farthest reaches of space and the innermost secrets of the atom. We travel along concrete roads and ingest processed food. So if we do not consciously stop and deliberately focus on God, it is very easy to begin to think that we really are masters of all we survey.

The university environment is an extension and in some ways a magnification of our human-made plastic world. We create a place where we can think and explore and gain skills that will be of use later. Meals are prepared. Activities are provided. Maintenance and cleaning chores are kept to a minimum in order to provide the opportunity for concentrated study that is not possible with all manner of other duties and distractions. But if we are not careful the campus environment can lead to a false sense of self-sufficiency and self-importance. If we do not stop to hear God's voice we will probably miss it. If we do not seek direction from beyond ourselves we are unlikely to find it.

It is one of those ironies that so many persons — given an environment that lends itself perfection to spiritual disciplines and self-examination — drift away from any spiritual discipline during the university experience. It no longer seems relevant. Maybe they've been turned off by the cultural idea of religion as simplistic moral platitudes or entertainment or personality cult. After all, few churches can compete with VH1, and many professors are more articulate than the hometown preacher. But more is at stake. Establishing a close and firm relationship with the only one worthy of praise and worship is far from irrelevant; it is the most important thing any of us can do. As old Reverend Donoway used to quote: "Ascribe to the Lord the glory of his name! Bring an offering, and come into the courts of the Lord. Worship the Lord in holy splendor!"

Responsibility And Motivation

Ruth 1:16

> *Where you go, I will go;*
> *Where you lodge, I will lodge;*
> *your people shall be my people,*
> *and your God my God.*

This passage from Ruth 1, so often read at contemporary weddings, conjures up mental images of a winsome and warmhearted love story that explains how Ruth, a Moabite woman, became an ancestor of the revered King David and, later, of Jesus of Nazareth. It is a simple story that dates back to an early period in the history of Israel, the era of the Judges. But it is an early and simple story that became very important in a later and more complex time, the time of Ezra and Nehemiah. That was the age when conflicts arose between Jews returning to their homeland after the Babylonian exile and Jews who had remained behind, in many cases intermarrying with Canaanites and becoming assimilated in the local culture. Tough questions arose about what it meant to be a Jew and hardliners looked suspiciously at foreigners and spoke against intermarriage. So this story, already old by that time, a story about a foreigner, Ruth, who was caught in circumstances she could not control and came to be not just an Israelite but part of the house of David, had a clear and timely message. It is a story that revolves around the importance of being willing to assume responsibility *and* the motivation for doing so.

A famine in their homeland of Judah had driven Elimelech, his wife Naomi, and their two sons to emigrate from Bethlehem, across the Jordan to the land of Moab, which was always more fertile than Palestine. In time, all three men — father and two sons, each of whom had married a Moabite woman — died, leaving Naomi with her two daughters-in-law, Ruth and Orpah. Seeing no future for a widow in a foreign land, Naomi decided to return to Judah and urged Orpah and Ruth likewise to return to their families who would care for them. It was in some ways a tender moment: they kissed, wept, and the young women insisted on accompanying Naomi. But Naomi did not want them. She had troubles enough of her own without having a couple of foreigners in tow. Orpah was eventually persuaded to follow her mother-in-law's advice. Ruth, however, persisted. "Where you go, I will go; Where you lodge, I will lodge; your people shall be my people, and your God my God."

She *made the choice* to cast her lot with Naomi and in effect to become responsible for the older woman whom she would be accompanying. Note that it is not as though Naomi wanted her. The text does not say that Naomi was pleased by this turn of events, merely that when she saw how determined Ruth was, she kept quiet. But while Naomi didn't particularly want this companionship, she may have needed it. Some commentators have suggested that without the younger woman's help, Naomi would probably not have survived the journey.

When they arrived back in Bethlehem, it became clear that sentimentality aside, the going would be rough. Ruth's words would be put to the test, because the young woman had to support Naomi and herself with backbreaking work, gleaning in the fields. How quickly the seemingly warm emotion of that familiar scene with Naomi, Ruth, and Orpah faded. An embittered Naomi complained to the women of Bethlehem: "I went away full," she said, "but the Lord has brought me back empty ..." (Ruth 1:21). How that statement must have hurt Ruth! Did she count for nothing? Naomi, who had not wanted Ruth's help or companionship, was obviously not all that grateful for it.

But Ruth had chosen to be responsible for Naomi, and stuck by that decision, which leads to the question, "What was her motivation?" She really could, after all, have gone home. It does not seem to have been the need to be needed or the desire to be appreciated, since she was neither. But she had made a choice and was now willing to live with its obligations. "Your people shall be my people, *and your God my God*," sounds a lot like a religious conversion. Ruth had come to recognize the God of Elimelech's family as the God of her life. She had learned of this God who had seen the distress of the Israelites in Egypt and come to their aid. She now worshiped the same God who would not allow Cain to evade responsibility by asking, "Am I my brother's keeper?" Of course he was! So it was this faith in the Hebrew God that led to her insistence on staying with Naomi: "... Your people shall be my people, and your God my God."

Could Ruth really have foreseen the situation into which her new faith would lead her? Of course not. No more than any young couple can really foresee what life will bring when they make warm and loving commitments at the altar, perhaps reciting the words of Ruth 1:16. No more than any person can really see what it will mean when they commit themselves to Jesus Christ and the Church. No one can fully see the future with its promises and challenges. But when we commit ourselves to God and to living according to godly principles we may not know what the future holds but, as the cliché says, we know who holds the future.

At this point in the story of Ruth and Naomi another key player enters: Boaz, the wealthy landowner in whose fields Ruth is gleaning who, the narrator tells us and Naomi soon enough realizes, is kin to Naomi's deceased husband. The whole fabric of life in ancient Israel was based on the integrity of the extended family or clan and there were regulations about mutual responsibility. While the details of these regulations are not clear (Deuteronomy 25: 5-6, Leviticus 25:25, and so on) it is plain that Boaz held some responsibility for Ruth and Naomi, but did not realize it. In the familiar nighttime scene on the threshing floor, Ruth informed Boaz that he was her next of kin and challenged him to exercise his rights and "take her under his wing" (Ruth 3:9). Essentially, Ruth was proposing marriage to Boaz. While it may have technically been his *responsibility*, it remained for Boaz to make the *choice to be responsible*. Again we ask the question, "What was his motivation for responsibility?"

In our modern world we focus so much on "romantic love" that it is virtually impossible to read this story without assuming that Boaz fell head over heels in love with the ravishingly beautiful

Ruth! This line of thought would never have occurred to the biblical community, just as it would not occur to many persons in the world today. The basis for marriage was not primarily romantic love, but the integrity of the community and the larger good of society. Hopefully, of course, love and fulfillment would be found within marriage.

This reminds us that we modern Americans have focused so much on the rights of the individual, on the need for each of us to "become our own person" and "have our own space," that we tend to overlook inherent family and community responsibilities. Spouses physically desert one another and abandon their children, adults sometimes physically, emotionally, or financially abandon their aging parents. Children are regularly neglected or abused. Clearly we need to be reminded that there are obligations inherent in family and societal life of which we may be as unaware as Boaz was of his obligation to Ruth. There need to be advocates — perhaps you and I — who are willing to be as bold as Ruth was in that midnight hour and say, "You have an obligation to others, not just yourself, and we will help you make the proper choice."

The story of Ruth arrives at a happy ending, but not without one more twist. There is, it turns out, another kinsman who is more directly related to Naomi and Ruth than Boaz. He was interested in acquiring the dead man's inheritance, but not the responsibility of caring for his wife and children that she might bear. So he passed up his obligation; he made the negative choice not to be responsible. Of all the characters who play a role of any significance in the book of Ruth, this kinsman, actually a closer relative than Boaz, is the only one who is not named. I have always felt the narrator is thereby telling us that this man, who did not want to shoulder the responsibility that was rightfully his, is not worth remembering.

Do I even need to ask what his short-sighted and selfish motivations were? Unlike Ruth, he does not seem to have caught the vision of the God of Israel; nor, like Boaz, did he understand his responsibility to the larger society around him. Instead he represents all those unnamed, often unidentified, influences that whisper in our ear that we can take but not give, that we can evade obligation and responsibility. And, of course, we can. But when we do, our families, our society, and the world are the poorer, and we become one of the no-names not worth remembering.

We are engaged in some great debates in our nation today, debates to which the little story of Ruth speaks with surprising clarity. There are those in our country who are as firm as Naomi about the need for foreigners to go back from where they came. We need to be reminded that some of these outsiders might have a clearer vision of that to which God is calling us than do we. Many are rightly concerned about trimming government fat and deficit reduction, but if we are in any measure a country with a Judeo-Christian base, as we like to say, we need to recall that we, like Boaz in the story of Ruth, have an obligation to hold the fabric of society together by somehow providing for the basic needs of others. This pushes all kinds of hot buttons: welfare, national health insurance, extended unemployment benefits, social security. I am sure there were some people in ancient Israel who felt that the provisions for gleaning were excessively generous and deprived landowners like Boaz of their fundamental right to their crops. But there has to be *some* system for providing for the basic needs of people. That is an inherent responsibility of society. We can certainly debate what system is best, but ultimately like Boaz and his unnamed relative, we can choose to meet or reject that responsibility.

As we chart a responsible future for ourselves and for our nation, we must be mindful of succumbing to the wrong motivation. If our desire is to be wanted and needed and appreciated, we are likely to be disillusioned; if it is to be faithful to the God of Israel and Jesus Christ, we are more likely to succeed. If we think that making the right choice will make us healthy, wealthy, and wise or match us up with Prince Charming, we may be disappointed.

Like all of us, Ruth had the opportunity to accept or reject responsibility in which motivation was the key. She made a choice based on faith in the God of Israel which obligated her to remain with Naomi and support the older woman. Her ultimate success was dependent upon Boaz acknowledging his obligation to care for her and, unlike the unnamed relative, shouldering it. What choices have you made in your life that have brought you responsibilities which you can not have foreseen, but which are very real and very challenging? Are there responsibilities that you should shoulder that you are trying to avoid, perhaps following the bad example of the anonymous crowd? Are you living out the responsibilities you undertook when you chose to follow Jesus Christ as Lord and Savior? "Where you go, I will go; Where you lodge, I will lodge; your people shall be my people, and your God my God."

Whose Values Are Your Values?

Mark 6:53—7:8

Joshua Lawrence Chamberlain was Professor of Rhetoric at Bowdoin College in Maine at the outbreak of the Civil War. A graduate of Bowdoin and Bangor Theological Seminary he, like many Northerners, was very much opposed to slavery. His conviction that all persons were created by God and equal in God's sight had been nurtured during his undergraduate years at Bowdoin through contact with a professor's wife who was working on a novel and discussing its progress with groups of students. The book was *Uncle Tom's Cabin*. She was Harriet Beecher Stowe.

After the war broke out, Chamberlain determined that the best way he could live out this deeply held value of human equality was to enlist in the Union Army. While the faculty at Bowdoin presumably shared his anti-slavery sentiment, they turned down his request for a leave of absence to enlist in the Union forces. They felt that his presence on campus was more important than a role he could play in the military. Undaunted, Chamberlain applied for a two-year study leave, which was readily granted. What he decided to study was how to serve in the Union Army.

As a university trained individual, Chamberlain was commissioned a Lieutenant Colonel in the Union forces and eventually put in command of the 20th Maine Volunteers. Unlike most commanders, who were either regular military men or West Point graduates, Chamberlain had neither specific training nor practical military experience. He was keenly aware of these deficiencies, and tried to make up for them by extensive reading on military strategy.

The 20th Maine ended up being part of the great Union force that stumbled upon the advancing Confederate Army at Gettysburg, Pennsylvania, on July 1, 1863. As the great and terrible battle progressed, it fell to Colonel Chamberlain and his already weary forces to defend the very end of the Union line at a strategic location called Little Round Top. "Hold that ground at all hazards," he was ordered. The battle was not going especially well for the 20th Maine. Outmanned and outgunned, they were almost out of ammunition when Colonel Chamberlain determined a course of action about which he had read in one of his volumes of military strategy: they would charge. While it may have been an act of desperation, it was not a willy-nilly, disorganized charge. It was a sophisticated and rare maneuver. The 20th Maine surprised the advancing Confederate forces by charging in hand to hand combat, in what Chamberlain described as "an extended right wheel," the troops proceeding like a door on a hinge, gradually penning their opponents in. It was a totally unexpected strategy. The fighting was fierce. In his official report on the battle he wrote, "An officer fired his pistol at my head with one hand, while he handed me his sword with the other."

I am not a Civil War buff nor a fan of warfare and violence of any kind. But I begin this academic year with this story because it illustrates a couple of things. It is a story of a person motivated by a deeply held religious value — the equality and dignity of all persons. And it is a story of how Chamberlain stood up to some very strong pressures not to put that value into practice: pressure first to stay on campus and steer clear of the fighting, and later, of course, fierce pressure at Little Round Top that resulted in extraordinary action.

It was a very different kind of struggle — a different sort of ideological and theological war, if you will — in which Jesus and the disciples were engaged in Mark 7. As practicing Jews, good faithful people, they encountered strong pressure to live out their religious commitment and their relationship with God in some very specific, culturally acceptable ways, namely by following the so-called "tradition of the elders." These were, as you may know, the over 600 regulations for keeping the Law of Moses which the Pharisees had devised involving, among other things, ritual purity. These laws about keeping cooking pots and serving vessels ritually clean are summed up in the old proverb, "Cleanliness is next to godliness." The trouble is that this kind of external cleanliness is not only *not* next to godliness, according to Jesus it may actually inadvertently steer us away from God by diverting us from life's real battles.

In today's Gospel story is one of those little details that we may very well skip over, but a little detail that opens our eyes to what is going on. At the end of Mark 6 there was a frenzy to get near Jesus for healing. Crowds were carrying the sick and disabled to Jesus, leaving them in the market place and begging Jesus to touch them. The narrative then says that the sick "begged him that they might even touch the *fringe* of his cloak," and that those who *did* touch the fringe were healed. This fringe was the twisted blue threads at the four corners of a male garment, still a part of Jewish prayer shawls, that were a constant reminder of God's commandments. The fact that Jesus wore this fringe shows that he too was a faithful observer of the Law of Moses. We see him wearing it in this sea of needy people who were begging for and receiving healing, wholeness, and salvation. The Law of Moses, symbolized by the blue fringe, propelled Jesus into the world to do God's will and show God's love.

It was a very different understanding of the law of God that kept many of the religious leaders away from the needy common people who, as today's lesson underscores, they regarded as being unclean. Modern biblical archaeology has reminded us of what is perhaps obvious: the religion Jesus attacks in today's lesson was largely an elitist, rich person's faith. These were those who had the time and money to spend on elaborate rituals and to keep multiple sets of dishes and pots, special vessels for cleansing, and to build separate ritual baths for men and woman as part of their homes. The problem was not that they had means to do these things, but that they were trying to please God while cutting themselves off from the majority of the people. Their faith had become self-centered rather than centered on God and neighbor, values fundamental to the Law of Moses, as Jesus reminded them when he summarized the law, "You shall love the Lord your God with all you heart and all your soul and all your mind and all your strength, and you shall love your neighbor as yourself." No wonder Jesus quoted the prophet Isaiah, "This people honors me with their lips, but their hearts are far from me."

Jesus went on to give a very specific example of the way the law of God was being twisted so that its central value was obscured. The fifth commandment about honoring your father and mother is often misunderstood today as if it were addressed to little kiddies. In fact, in its original context it was clearly addressed to adults. In a society with no pensions or old folks' homes everybody understood what it meant to honor parents: it meant to care for them in their old age. But some were claiming that the savings or possessions that should have been used to support their elderly parents were "Corban," that is, dedicated to God. This practice seemed to justify their doing nothing for their parents in God's name. Jesus said that in spite of their public display of piety, they were ignoring the clear intent of the Law of Moses. The values they proclaimed — faithfulness to God, righteousness, obedience — were not really their values at all. Their real values were self-serving, not God serving. They were saying one thing and doing another.

Is this not just the sort of thing which has soured so many modern Americans? They look at government and see a legislator who votes for a campaign reform bill knowing full well that it will never make it out of conference committee. That way he or she can claim to support the concept without having to live with the consequences. They look at a philanthropy and find that funds given to aid the destitute have been diverted to promote the lavish lifestyle of the executive director or to pay hush money to keep a scandal under wraps. They look at an employee who has given decades of service to a corporation, fired just before he is eligible for early retirement, left without a paycheck or health insurance. They look at the church and see a group that talks about brotherly love, but is torn apart by gossip and innuendo.

That politician may really believe in campaign reform in principle, but it is not really his value. The fund-raiser may have so convinced himself or herself that personal good and the charity's good are synonymous, and so forth. It is not enough to tip the hat to values like loyalty, honesty, love, and acceptance. What matters is, whose values are your values? How do we really act? Are your real values God-serving or self-serving?

We live in a world no less needy than Gennerseret. Oh, the needs may be different, but there are people all around us crying out for help and healing. We hear the cries face to face, in the newspaper or on television. We see the need in the downcast look that is not put into words. We, like Jesus and the disciples, can be propelled into this world of need by God's love, led by God's spirit; or we can use a parody of Christianity as an escape from the world, just as those Jesus challenged used the "tradition of the elders" as an escape from real life responsibility. You can disengage, become self-absorbed, self-centered and, if you aren't careful, self-satisfied and smug in your faith, just like those with whom Jesus contended. I see both happen every year: students who grow and students who become ingrown. Jesus and the disciples found themselves in the midst of a needy, clamoring world, feeding, teaching, and healing. The Pharisees were there too. They despised the common folk because they were unclean and wanted to keep themselves pure.

Joshua Lawrence Chamberlain was awarded the Congressional Medal of Honor for his valor at Little Round Top. He went on to fight in many major battles and to be wounded three times, on one occasion being pronounced mortally wounded by the field surgeon. But he lived and ended the war as a Brigadier General. Later in life he served four terms as Governor of Maine and for a time was President of Bowdoin College. But we know from his diaries and letters that he always looked back to that day on a rocky spot in Pennsylvania as the defining moment in his life. It was at the instant that the value he said was most important to him — fundamental human equality — was put to the ultimate test.

You will be tested every day. You will have the opportunity to be engaged, in one way or another, in a real world that needs the best and most courageous action you can muster. You will also have the opportunity to seek refuge from that world. Every day you will have the chance to define the moment or to be defined by it: you will have the opportunity to show whose values are *really* your values.

More Than Sex

Song of Solomon 2:8-16a, 8:6-7; 1 John 3:11-23; John 15:12-17

> *My beloved speaks and says to me:*
> *"Arise, my love, my fair one, and come away;*
> *for now the winter is past,*
> *the rain is over and gone.*
> *...*
> *Arise, my love, my fair one, and come away.*
> *O my dove, in the clefts of the rock,*
> *in the covert of the cliff,*
> *let me see your face, let me hear your voice;*
> *for your voice is sweet,*
> *and your face is lovely."*
> *My beloved is mine and I am his ...*
> — Song of Solomon 2:10-16a

Every summer, like many university chaplains, I am part of a number of weddings of University of Evansville graduates. One of the things that I enjoy about these weddings is that often they are not the traditional brief and nondescript Protestant wedding "ceremonies," but truly services of worship, a "setting of seals" in the context of Christian worship, certainly the appropriate context for the binding together of two persons.

It has interested me that at several of these worship services in the past two or three years, one of the scripture readings has been from chapter 2 of the Song of Solomon. A year ago I was invited to preach on this text at a wedding, and the mother of the bride called to express her concern over what I might say, because she was a Sunday School teacher and UMW President and she knew that *this book is about sexuality*. You don't have to be a private detective to figure out why, in the text quoted at these weddings and which I read a moment ago, the young man is standing outside the wall, gazing at the windows and looking through his beloved's lattice and whispering to her. He can hardly wait to be with her, and the feelings are clearly mutual! That is why, when the Jewish rabbis met in Jamnia in 90 A.D. to set the canon of the Hebrew Bible, there was such great debate over whether such a steamy document should be included. But cool heads prevailed and it was, for two reasons, one of which is very much in keeping with the spirit of our times, and one of which is not; but both of which I suspect at least some couples understand.

The first reason the Song of Solomon made it into the canon is that it *is* about sexuality and sexuality is a good, God-given gift. This is the part of the argument that twentieth century Americans understand. Sex must be good — we talk and think about it all the time and use it to market everything. Of course the assumption of the Song, like the assumption of the whole Bible, is that sexuality is a good, God-given gift that will be exercised appropriately, non-exploitively, within the bonds of monogamous, life-long marriage.

But there are non-sexual passages too: "Set me as a seal upon your heart, as a seal upon your arms; for love is as strong as death, *passion* fierce as the grave" (Song of Solomon 8:6-7).

Here is the second reason that the Song made it into the canon: because the rabbis, like generations of Jews and Christians ever since, recognized that the Song is about sexuality *and more*. It is about *love and passion and devotion*, three things which our reductionist society doesn't handle nearly as well as it does sex.

Just over 860 years ago, Abbot Bernard began to preach a series of sermons from the Song of Solomon to his fellow monks at Clairvaux in France. Over the next nineteen years, he preached 86 sermons from this book, and got less than half way through the text. Writing about chapter 2, Saint Bernard knew that the literal meaning of the bride's words were that her groom, standing and looking in through the windows of the wall, was restrained by modesty and social custom from coming in. But the celibate monk also knew there is more to life and relationships than sex. He heard in these poetic words of one person's love for another, the echoes of his own relationship with God.

The spiritual sense of this text, he said, is what happens when we, as individual members of the Bride of Christ, the Church, are approached by the Bridegroom, our spiritual spouse, Jesus Christ. There is a wall that impedes his approach into our lives, the wall of sin — human barriers that we construct that keep God at a distance. We have our moments — there are lattices and windows through which we sense the presence of God — but barriers keep us from full union with Christ. Yet it is that knowledge that the lover is there, so near and yet so unattainable, that only increases our longing. "Our hearts," Saint Augustine had observed, "are restless until they find their rest in Thee," in God.

There are two things that clearly follow from Bernard's insights into the Song of Solomon. First, when feelings are so intense, longings so deep and devotion so great, they will have to be expressed somehow. Now, we all know that people are different and express their feelings in a variety of ways. Some couples are very demonstrative in showing their affection — almost embarrassingly so, I might say; others are quite reserved, writing notes or poetry to one another. But we are quite properly concerned when two persons are engaged to be married and seem to have no passion for one another. We fear that the marriage may be one of convenience, perhaps providing an escape from an unfortunate homelife. I need not even mention what happens to a marriage when the passion dies.

Similarly, some persons express their love for God in very demonstrative and energetic ways — ways that may make others a little uncomfortable — while others express their devotion through deeper prayer, longer meditation, or more intense intellectual struggles. *But* if there is *no* passion, there is reason for concern. John Wesley, the founder of the Methodist movement, knew of the problems that occur when one goes through the motions of religion without the love and devotion of which Scripture speaks. This "poor scrap" of religion is "like she who fancies herself a virtuous woman, only because she is not a prostitute; or him who dreams he is an honest man, merely because he does not rob or steal. May the Lord God of my fathers preserve me from such a poor, starved religion as this." In other words, a *passionless* religion.

I am sure that some of you know about the Frog Follies that comes to Evansville every year. It is a hot-rod show that takes up just about all the hotel space in the area and is usually the same weekend that freshmen move into UE. While I am not personally involved in restoring old hot-rods, it is impressive to see the time, energy, and money — the passion — that persons invest in this activity. Sometimes whole families are involved in fixing them up, cleaning them out, refinishing the bodies, and restoring these vehicles to mint condition — in some cases better than mint. As Christian people, we are called by Jesus Christ to restore the world, in a process that is not too unlike restoring an old car. Racism, oppression, and poverty — sins — are like the dents and scratches in the old auto body. Just as through months and years of effort and investment the old car can be restored to mint condition, when we experience the love and grace of God in our lives — when we feel the passion — we are drawn to do all we can to restore the world to the way God created it to be — a world where all the parts are in place and the needs of people come first.

The poetic Wesley brother, Charles, addressed the same issue in verse:

> *Ye different sects, who all declare,*
> *"Lo, here is Christ!" or, "Christ is there!"*
> *Your stronger proofs divinely give,*
> *And show me where the Christians live.*

We can tell ourselves and others that we love God, that we are religious people, a faith community, a godly nation for a host of reasons, many of them self-serving and self-deceptive. But if this love doesn't show one way or the other — if there is no passion for God — there is cause for concern.

The second thing that follows from Saint Bernard is that we are reminded that true love always expands us, makes us bigger people, and draws others into our lives. The Song of Solomon is not a private communication violated by our prying eyes. As intense as it is, it is a public document, addressed to friends, inviting them to join in the couple's joy. This is, of course, the theme which is underscored in the Gospel and letters of John.

Some of you have probably heard about the city in Latin America where pellets of medical cobalt waste were inappropriately disposed in a landfill and ended up being mixed with gravel and spread throughout the town. The landfill workers received the tragic news: they had received lethal doses of radiation and were dying. The townspeople were frightened. The cobalt pellets were like land mines hidden on their streets, waiting for the children to play with them. The workers met and made a dramatic decision: they were as good as dead, so they volunteered to find the pellets and save the children. I don't know whether there was any religious motivation in their decision; but it is clear that their tragedy expanded their horizons and allowed them to tap inner strength. This is the expansion, the empowerment that results when one feels the intensity of God's love in Jesus Christ: one will be friend to others, one cannot help having expanded horizons and changed views of others.

Many Christians today find Saint Bernard's approach, the anagogic reading of Scripture, to be far-fetched, even ludicrous. I think Saint Bernard knew what we forget: that there is something even more passionate and powerful than the sexual love between a man and a woman, and that is the love between God and a human soul. We are reminded that as human beings, we are bundles of longings; we long to be loved and appreciated; we long to be needed; most of all we long to be in relationship with our family, with a meaningful community, with a significant other and with God.

When our Lord commands us to "love one another," (John 15:17) it is not simply bestowing a blessing upon the natural impulses we feel toward a few select individuals. It is rather to be so grounded in our love for God, and to be so secure in the love and relationship of friends in community, that we can "go and bear fruit, fruit that will last" (John 15:16). In the last analysis, it is this deep love for God and for others — with all love's passion and devotion — that makes it possible for us to venture out in love and service to all, as Jesus commanded.

What Kind Of Love?

1 John 4:7-10

A generation ago, C. S. Lewis set out to write a book on love, using as his main text: "God is Love" from 1 John 4:

> *Beloved, let us love one another, because love is from God; everyone who loves is born of God and knows God. Whoever does not love does not know God, for God is love. God's love was revealed among us in this way: God sent his only Son into the world so that we might live through him. In this is love, not that we loved God but that he loved us and sent his Son to be the atoning sacrifice for our sins.* — 1 John 4:7-10

His plan, he later revealed, was a simple one. He would divide the various human emotions we tend to lump together as love into two categories: Need-love and Gift-love. Need-love, in Lewis' system, was fundamentally self-centered and self-serving, meeting our own needs. Gift-love, on the other hand, would follow the pattern of the Divine Love manifested in God's self-emptying in the Incarnation: giving without regard for reciprocation.

I am sure that many sermons have been preached on this distinction between superficial and self-centered need-love and more profound, other-focused gift love, disparaging the first and exalting the second. The problem, as Lewis discovered, is that this is a false dichotomy. Needs are not necessarily superficial or selfish, and gifts are not necessarily altruistic. In the Genesis creation story, after God created the archetypal person, God looked at Adam and said, "It is not good for the human being to be alone," and so created another. Human needs come built in; they are neither defects nor flaws.

We know from everyday experience how this tension works. We sometimes engage in good works, giving blood or helping with flood relief, out of pure altruism. But it is just as often because we hope that if we are ever in such need, similar help with be forthcoming. We are almost always drawn to acquaintances, friends, and spouses both because of who they are in themselves and because of the way they meet our needs. Sometimes we are drawn to persons quite different from ourselves to compliment our strengths and make up for our weaknesses. "Opposites attract!" people say. At other times we are drawn to those who share our interests, our outlooks, and our Christian commitment: "Oh, they're like two peas in a pod!"

Almost all relationships are a combination of both: reinforcement in some areas and complimenting in others. In marriage more than in any other human relationship, our human needs to give and to receive, to love and to be loved, to be appreciated and to be grateful are present constantly. There are few things worse, the pop psychologists tell us, than for a marriage to become "one sided" with one partner always giving, the other always receiving, one's needs constantly met, the other's consistently ignored. It is not good, as the Bible teaches, for a person to be alone, physically, emotionally, spiritually, or psychologically alone.

If it is true — and it is — that much of what we romantically call love has to do more with meeting needs, mutual gratification, and support, then exactly where does gift-love, patterned after the divine gift of God, fit into relationships, to marriage? It is crucial at two points. We display gift-love on those occasions when we are able to detach ourselves, our own needs and desires, and simply seek that which is best for the beloved. A few years ago I visited an acquaintance, a pastor from Central America, who had just completed a year long fellowship of graduate study in Indianapolis. I was surprised to learn that his family was remaining in the United States a second year, at considerable hardship, while his wife completed her bachelor's degree, a process she had interrupted when they married over a decade earlier. "So many men in our region," he said, "progress in their careers and education, and the wife just follows along. I wanted Claudia to have the opportunity to do this." Particularly in marriage, which is after all a very complex partnership, it is important sometimes to give unequivocal gifts, just for the other.

The second crucial role of gift-love, as indelicate as it may be to bring up in the middle of a wedding, is the divine gift-love that enables us to love that which is not naturally lovable, and we all have unlovable parts and our unlovable times. I know of nothing more honest than the Christian wedding vows: for better, for *worse*; for richer, for *poorer;* in *sickness* and in health. For all those things that are lovable, and the things that aren't so lovable too.

As a rule I don't know what about the couples I marry is unlovable — and I'm happy that way! But I am sure that there is something in each of them as there is in all of us that can be loved only by patience, kindness, forbearance, forgiveness, and grace — by Divine gift-love — by all those things mentioned in 1 Corinthians 13.

"Beloved, let us love one another," our modern translations of 1 John read. They could equally well say, "Let us love amongst ourselves," awkward grammar, but a good thought. A marriage is truly blessed when there are all kinds of love in the mix of things: need-love that gratifies and fulfills; gift-love that regards the other as a truly unique and important individual; and divine gift-love that gives us such forgiveness and grace that we can love and accept even those things in others that are unlovable. My prayer for couples joined in marriage, and all they touch over the years, is that that they may always love amongst themselves.

www.ingramcontent.com/pod-product-compliance
Lightning Source LLC
Chambersburg PA
CBHW071730040426
42446CB00011B/2299